VELOCITY, MOMENTUM & DISTRIBUTION

THE THREE FORCES BEHIND SUSTAINABLE STARTUP GROWTH

EDIDIONG EKONG

Edidiong speaks directly to builders. In a world chasing hype, this book reminds us that real momentum comes from consistency and systems. It's practical, grounded, and deeply relevant for anyone serious about building something that lasts.
— *Abidemi Adesokan, Head of Growth, Nomba (YC '19)*

Edidiong cuts through the noise when he writes, delivering the message so succinctly that you can tell it is grounded in undeniable expertise and experience. This book offers a clear, authoritative, and verifiable recipe for startup growth.
— *Kelechi Ibe, Co-founder & CEO, TaxStreem*

The book demystifies growth, showing that it isn't magic or luck, but the result of deliberate decisions, disciplined execution, and systems that compound progress over time. It is a practical guide for leaders serious about building sustainable scale.
— *Dele Kadiri, GM, Boomplay*

What sets Edidiong apart is his ability to translate complex growth principles into a structured, scalable framework. This book reveals how sustainable value is engineered through discipline and smart execution. Founders and executives alike will find long-term thinking embedded in every chapter.
— *Rodolpho (Rudi) Ribeiro, Marketing Expert (Ex. Fireflies, Nothing, Deezer)*

In a world obsessed with overnight success, this book is a refreshing reminder that real growth comes from consistency and systems. It provides practical, actionable insight for founders who want sustainable momentum, not just quick wins.

— *Peace Itimi, CEO Rivva (Ex. Smile Identity, HoaQ Ventures, Seedstars, Korapay)*

In this powerful work, Edidiong dismantles the myth that growth is accidental. With clarity and strategic depth, they demonstrate how disciplined systems and intentional leadership create enduring success. This is not just a book—it's a powerful guide for leaders building institutions that last.

— *Achille Cossi, CEO & Co-founder Bujeti (YC '23)*

In the digital era, scalable systems determine success. Edidiong presents a modern, forward-thinking framework that captures the mechanics of sustainable growth. This book belongs on every technology leader's desk.

— *Christian Jombo, VP of Technology, Kora (Techstars '19)*

To everyone building something that truly matters.

The founder asking whether today's decisions will compound or collapse.

The operator turning chaos into systems, while others chase headlines.

The investor looking for real signal beneath the noise.

This is for you.

Table Of Contents

Introduction:

The Forces That Actually Drive Growth

There is a pervasive fantasy in startup culture that success arrives suddenly, delivered by some combination of brilliant insight, perfect timing, and algorithmic fortune that borders on providence. A founder has an idea, builds a product, achieves the mythical product-market fit, and watches as growth compounds exponentially until the company becomes the next unicorn celebrated in headlines and case studies. This narrative is so deeply embedded in how we talk about startups that it shapes how founders think about building companies, how investors evaluate opportunities, and how the media covers the technology industry.

The fantasy is seductive, precisely because it contains fragments of truth. Companies do sometimes experience periods of exponential growth. Products occasionally find immediate resonance with large markets. Distribution sometimes occurs through mechanisms that appear highly efficient. Yet the narrative obscures far more than it reveals, leading founders to optimize for the wrong things, chase the wrong opportunities, and build companies on foundations that cannot support sustainable scale.

The reality behind nearly every overnight success is years of methodical work that occurs largely outside public view.

Growth is not a discrete event that happens to you; it is a system you build deliberately. It emerges through the interaction of three forces: how quickly progress compounds (velocity), how strongly it persists (momentum), and how effectively it propagates through a market (distribution). These forces operate consistently across contexts, though their specific manifestations vary dramatically; a nuance that will become clear in the chapters ahead.

Why This Book Exists

Most discussions of startup growth focus on tactics rather than systems, on what to do rather than how to think, and on optimizing metrics rather than building mechanisms that generate lasting advantage. Founders are bombarded with advice about which channels to use, which metrics to track, and which playbooks to follow based on what worked for other companies in different contexts.

This book exists to shift that focus. It is designed to help you see growth not as a series of isolated campaigns or hacks, but as a dynamic system. A system where decisions compound, where choices interact over time, and where building the right foundations matters more than chasing quick wins.

At its core, this book is about alignment: reframing growth from something to chase into a system to engineer. The most successful companies are not the luckiest or the most talented, but the most deliberate in how they build sustainable growth.

What Makes This Book Different

Many growth frameworks focus on optimizing isolated variables: acquisition channels, conversion rates, or viral loops. This book treats growth as a dynamic system. Changes in one part of the system influence others; some effects compound, some decay, and all interact in ways that determine long-term outcomes.

You will not find growth hacks or secret tactics here. You will have a coherent theory of how velocity creates momentum, how momentum enables distribution, and how distribution turns small initial advantages into compounding returns.

By the end of this book, you will be able to:

- Diagnose stalled growth and identify underlying causes.
- Assess whether your organization is building sustainable advantages or generating temporary traction.
- Make strategic choices about where to invest time, resources, and attention for long-term impact.

This book provides frameworks, not checklists. It will help you think differently about growth, whether you are a founder, product leader, marketer, or investor.

Who Should Read This Book

This book is written primarily for founders building companies, but the frameworks and principles apply to anyone responsible for growth. Product leaders, marketing leaders, and investors will find frameworks for assessing whether startups are building sustainable advantages or just generating temporary traction through tactics that do not scale.

This is not a book for readers seeking shortcuts or validation that the path will be easy. It is for those willing to engage with the complex reality of how growth actually works rather than the simplified narratives. The difference between a temporary spike and compounding growth is not luck or genius, but understanding the structure beneath the surface.

The book assumes basic familiarity with startup concepts and terminology, but does not require deep expertise. Its goal is not to introduce, but to reframe how you think about it.

How to Read This Book

The book is organized as a sequential argument that builds across chapters, with each chapter introducing concepts that are developed further in subsequent chapters.

The first three chapters establish the core framework by examining the illusion of overnight success, defining velocity as the first advantage, and explaining how momentum is built rather than found. These chapters establish the conceptual foundation for subsequent chapters.

The middle chapters explore how products create compounding value, how positioning becomes self-reinforcing, and how distribution advantages accumulate over time. These chapters provide a detailed examination of the mechanisms by which momentum builds and competitive advantage emerges.

The later chapters focus on application: when to use patience and when to use urgency, how data and AI affect decision speed, and how teams create and sustain momentum. Here, the emphasis shifts from theory to execution.

The final chapter addresses playing the long game: how to scale without losing velocity, how to protect momentum as complexity increases, and how to build companies that endure through trust, ethics, and deliberate distribution strategy.

Throughout the book, concepts are illustrated with examples from real companies across categories and stages. These examples are not playbooks but illustrations of principles in action. The goal is not to copy tactics, but to understand the forces that made them effective and apply that reasoning to your own context.

To help you apply these frameworks directly, this book comes with a free practical toolkit: a companion workbook with chapter-by-chapter exercises, and a diagnostic scorecard that maps your company's position across velocity, momentum, and distribution. You will find details in the next section titled "Before You Begin". I recommend keeping the workbook open as you read; the frameworks compound fastest when you apply them to your own context in real time.

The Path Forward

Growth is not magic, luck, or genius, though all of those can help. Growth results from deliberate decisions, consistent execution, and the development of systems that amplify progress over time.

This is difficult work. It requires discipline, strategic clarity, and long-term thinking. It demands maintaining conviction when outcomes are uncertain and resisting the temptation to boost short-term metrics at the expense of durable value.

But this is also work that matters. Building companies that solve real problems creates value that compounds throughout the economy. Building products that people genuinely love makes their lives measurably better. Building organizations where talented people can do meaningful work creates opportunities that extend far beyond the company itself.

The opportunity is there for those willing to do the work. The rest is up to you.

Let us begin.

BEFORE YOU BEGIN: Your V∩M∩D Practical Toolkit

This book is designed to change how you think about growth. The toolkit below is designed to help you act on it.

THE V∩M∩D COMPANION WORKBOOK

A chapter-by-chapter exercise guide with more than 25 hands-on activities that turn the frameworks in this book into decisions for your company. For every chapter you read, there is a corresponding exercise waiting for you.

- Deconstruct your growth narrative and separate signal from noise
- Run a velocity audit on your team's actual shipping speed
- Design your company's specific momentum flywheel
- Map your owned versus rented distribution channels
- Architect an integrated growth system, not just campaigns
- Build a 90-day V∩M∩D priority plan for your weakest force

THE V∩M∩D DIAGNOSTIC SCORECARD

A 45-question self-assessment spreadsheet that scores your company across all three forces and shows you exactly where you sit in the V∩M∩D Venn diagram. Automated formulas calculate your position and track progress over time.

- Score yourself across nine subcategories of Velocity, Momentum, and Distribution
- See your V∩M∩D intersection on an automated dashboard
- Identify whether you are in V∩M, V∩D, M∩D, or the center
- Track your scores monthly and measure real progress
- Pinpoint your highest leverage gap with the subcategory breakdown

HOW TO ACCESS YOUR TOOLKIT

Scan the QR code below or visit:
www.edidiongekong.com/vmd-toolkit

Read each chapter, then open the workbook and apply it to your company. The frameworks only compound when you put them to work.

Chapter 1:

The Illusion of Overnight Success

What looks like a sudden arrival is almost always
the visible moment in a much longer arc of
compounding work that took place largely
outside of public view.

— James Clear, Atomic Habits

The Mythology of Sudden Arrival

Every successful startup arrives in the public consciousness as if by magic, creating a narrative that is both seductive and deeply misleading. One day, a company is unknown, operating in relative obscurity with a small user base and limited awareness. The next day, they are everywhere: featured in major publications, discussed on podcasts, analyzed by investors, and celebrated as the next inevitable success story. The media calls it hockey stick growth, a term that suggests a long period of flat progress followed by a sudden, almost vertical ascent. Investors call it product-market fit, that elusive moment when a product finds its natural place in the world and demand begins to compound. Founders call it validation, the external confirmation that their vision was correct all along. All of them describe the same phenomenon from different vantage points, yet they fundamentally miss the underlying truth.

The illusion of overnight success is seductive precisely because it suggests that greatness is accessible to anyone with a sufficiently good idea and a bit of luck, that the barriers to building something significant are lower than they actually are. In reality, this narrative is not just misleading; it is dangerous. It creates a fantasy world in which companies appear through brilliant ideas, perfect timing, or algorithmic luck, obscuring the more complex truth: true success is the result of sustained, compounding effort. Greatness is indeed accessible, but not through sudden breakthroughs or viral moments. It is accessible to those who understand the mechanics of compounding deeply enough to construct systems that generate it, who execute with relentless consistency over extended periods, and who build institutional capabilities rather than chasing individual moments of success.

Yet the myth persists because the media compresses years of work into a single dramatic story, showing only the visible moment of growth while hiding the long period of iteration, failure, and learning that preceded it. Social proof amplifies the effect: when a breakout success is widely celebrated, it convinces founders and teams that similar results are readily replicable. Cultural myths about heroic founders, flashes of inspiration, and "lucky" breakthroughs reinforce the notion that growth occurs suddenly, creating a seductive narrative in which anyone with the right idea or timing could achieve the same meteoric rise. These forces make the myth of overnight success feel not only possible, but inevitable, even though the reality is far more complex.

The Hidden Years Behind Visible Success

Consider Instagram, perhaps the quintessential example of apparent overnight success in the consumer technology landscape. The story most people know begins in October

2010, when a clean, elegant photo-sharing application appeared in the App Store and attracted 25,000 users on its first day. Within 2 months, it had one million users. Within 18 months, Facebook acquired it for $1 billion in a deal announced in April 2012, combining cash and stock. The trajectory seems impossibly steep, the kind of growth that suggests either genius or extraordinary fortune.

The story most people do not know is that Instagram was not the product of sudden inspiration or mere fortunate timing. It was the result of years of experimentation by founders who had already built and attempted to scale a location-based startup called Burbn. Burbn was an HTML5 mobile web app, inspired by Foursquare and Systrom's interest in bourbon whiskey, that enabled users to check in at locations, plan future visits, earn points, and post photos. It secured a $500,000 seed funding round from Baseline Ventures and Andreessen Horowitz while still in its prototype phase. Kevin Systrom and Mike Krieger had spent months trying to make Burbn work, adding features and testing hypotheses, before recognizing that users primarily engaged with one aspect of the application: the photo-sharing functionality. The clean, focused product that Apple featured and that millions adopted emerged only after the founders made the difficult decision to strip away almost everything they had built, focusing intensely on the single use case that showed genuine traction. The breakthrough came not from adding more but from subtracting almost everything, a process that required both courage and clarity about what actually mattered.

Slack provides another instructive example of how the visible moment of success conceals years of preparation and learning. When Slack launched to the public in 2014, it grew faster than perhaps any enterprise software product in history, reaching a billion-dollar valuation within 2 years. The narrative suggested that Stewart Butterfield and his team had somehow discovered a perfect product at a perfect moment. The reality was considerably more complex and more interesting. Slack was built by a team that had spent years developing Glitch, an ambitious multiplayer gaming company that ultimately failed to achieve sustainable traction in a crowded and challenging market. The internal communication tool they built to coordinate their distributed team while working on Glitch became the foundation for what would become Slack, but only after the team recognized that their game would not survive while their workflow software solved a genuine problem for teams everywhere. The "overnight" success of Slack was built on the accumulated experience, technical infrastructure, and hard-won insights from a failed gaming company.

Across industries, these stories illustrate a common structure: what looks sudden is always built on prior learning, iteration, and system design. Understanding that structure is key to growing any business.

Understanding the Underlying Structure

Stripe's path to dominance in online payments follows a similar pattern: long preparation precedes visible success. The payments infrastructure existed long before Patrick and John Collison wrote their first line of code. PayPal, Authorize.net, and numerous other processors had been facilitating online transactions for years. Stripe did not win by being first to market or even by having fundamentally different technology initially. They won by obsessing over developer experience in a way that no incumbent had prioritized, by removing every possible point of friction from the integration process, and by making the invisible complexity of financial infrastructure feel simple and elegant. That simplicity, which appeared effortless to the developers who integrated Stripe, required years of careful design, iterative refinement, and extensive technical work to implement properly.

The pattern repeats across industries, business models, and decades of startup history. What appears sudden to external observers is almost always the result of cumulative efforts by those building the company. Visibility arrives all at once, often triggered by an external catalyst such as a major funding round, a press feature, or reaching a usage threshold that makes growth self-evident. But the work behind it accumulates gradually over time, through countless iterations, experiments, failures, and incremental improvements that occur largely out of public view. Stripe's rise shows how deliberate, iterative work compounds quietly until the world finally takes notice.

The Consequences of Misunderstanding Growth

This fundamental confusion about how growth actually works produces predictable and damaging consequences throughout the startup ecosystem. Founders, taking their cues from the compressed narratives they read in TechCrunch or hear on podcasts, begin chasing viral mechanics instead of building sustainable systems. They optimize for launch moments rather than retention loops, believing that the right publicity at the right time will create momentum. Marketing leaders focus their energy on campaigns rather than compounding channels, seeking the big swing that will transform awareness rather than building assets that appreciate over time. Product teams optimize for features that will generate buzz at launch rather than for functionality that will keep users engaged over months and years. Everyone looks for the single tactic that will unlock exponential growth, and almost everyone misses the underlying structure that makes growth sustainable rather than ephemeral.

Growth is not a hack to be discovered or a secret to be unlocked through insider knowledge. It is not a lucky break or fortuitous timing, though timing certainly matters. Growth is fundamentally the result of three interconnected forces operating within a coherent system: velocity, momentum, and distribution.

The Three Forces of Sustainable Growth

Velocity represents the rate at which a company learns and ships, the fundamental speed of execution that determines how quickly a team can test ideas, iterate based on feedback, and close the gap between what they are building and what the market actually needs. Velocity is not merely about working long hours or moving quickly in some abstract sense. It is about the structure of decision-making, the tightness of feedback loops, and the ability to translate learning into action without unnecessary friction. Startups that achieve high velocity make more attempts over a given period, learn faster from each attempt, and adapt their approach before competitors fully understand what is changing in the market.

Momentum is what emerges when velocity becomes consistent and directional over time. Momentum is traction that persists beyond individual campaigns or temporary spikes in attention. It is the sensation that the business is working at a fundamental level, that growth is not random or dependent on heroic individual efforts, that each week builds meaningfully on the last. Momentum cannot be manufactured in a single quarter through clever marketing or aggressive spending. It emerges from repeated progress in the same direction, from compounding improvements that reinforce each other. Companies with genuine momentum do not need to convince the market that they are growing through press releases or carefully staged announcements. The growth becomes self-evident to anyone paying attention.

Distribution is the strategic architecture through which a product reaches users, retains them, and expands within accounts or networks. Distribution is not a marketing channel or a go-to-market plan, though it encompasses both. Distribution is the fundamental system that governs how a company acquires customers, retains them, and drives revenue growth. Distribution is why some products with demonstrably inferior features win their markets anyway, and why genuinely superior products sometimes fail in obscurity. Distribution, more than product quality or team talent, often determines which companies build lasting businesses and which ones remain interesting ideas that never scale.

How Growth Actually Works

The interaction among velocity, momentum, and distribution constitutes a reinforcing system in which each force amplifies the others. Velocity enables rapid experimentation with distribution channels and business models, creating more opportunities to find approaches that generate momentum. Momentum makes distribution more efficient because products that deliver genuine value generate word-of-mouth, retention provides a predictable foundation for planning acquisition investments, and market position attracts customers organically. Distribution advantages create more opportunities to learn and iterate, thereby increasing velocity and compounding momentum as network effects and market position strengthen.

Early-stage companies struggle primarily with velocity because they have not yet learned what drives growth. They need to iterate quickly on product-market fit, positioning, and channels. The constraint is learning speed, not usually capital or opportunity. Companies should optimize for velocity: small teams, flexible pivots, core focus, and rapid feedback. Once traction exists, the challenge shifts to building momentum: compounding early advantages into sustainable growth. Later, distribution becomes central for reaching customers efficiently and maintaining market position. These forces are interconnected: velocity without momentum is thrashing; momentum without distribution is a mirage; distribution without velocity is stagnation. Companies that scale sustainably align all three forces.

As companies reach scale, distribution becomes increasingly central to maintaining competitive advantages. They have product-market fit and operational momentum, but need systematic ways to reach customers efficiently as markets mature and competition intensifies. Distribution at scale requires approaches different from early-stage tactics: building content and brand that attract customers organically, developing partnerships and integrations that generate systematic referrals, optimizing complex multi-channel acquisition models in which different channels serve different segments, and leveraging data and technology to continuously increase efficiency. These three forces do not operate in isolation from each other. They form an interconnected system where each element enables and amplifies the others. Velocity without momentum is merely thrashing, lots of activity and motion that produces no consistent direction or compounding results.

Momentum without effective distribution is a mirage, creating the internal sensation of progress while failing to translate that progress into a sustainable market position. Distribution without velocity is stagnation, where a company has access to users but cannot improve quickly enough to retain them or expand the relationship over time. The companies that scale sustainably and build lasting value are those that align all three forces, creating a system in which speed of execution generates consistent traction, enables increasingly sophisticated distribution, and, in turn, demands even higher velocity to capitalize on the opportunities that distribution creates.

The game is not about going viral, generating buzz, or capturing temporary attention. The game is about building a machine that generates and captures value faster than the market can commoditize it, that gets stronger rather than weaker as it grows, that creates genuine barriers to competition through accumulated advantages. That requires velocity in execution. It requires momentum in results. It requires distribution as a strategy. Everything else, no matter how exciting or attention-grabbing it might be in the moment, is ultimately just noise.

🔍 *Case Study - Clubhouse*

When Viral Growth Masks Missing Foundations

The previous sections describe how sustainable growth emerges from the interaction of velocity, momentum, and distribution, and why apparent overnight success is almost always the visible surface of long, compounding work beneath the surface. But understanding a system fully requires examining not only its successes but also its failures, especially those that, at first glance, appear spectacular.

Clubhouse represents a rare and instructive case: a company that achieved extraordinary visibility and adoption without building the underlying forces that sustain durable growth. Its rise was not an illusion. Millions of people used the product intensely, but its foundations were incomplete. By examining Clubhouse through the lens of velocity, momentum, and distribution, we can see how explosive growth can mask structural weaknesses, delay necessary investments, and ultimately accelerate collapse once temporary conditions change. This is not a story about hype versus substance; it is a story about what happens when growth arrives before the system that sustains it.

In March 2020, as the world entered lockdown and millions of people found themselves isolated at home with unlimited time and an overwhelming need for human connection, a small audio-based social network called Clubhouse emerged from nowhere and captured the zeitgeist with unprecedented speed. The app allowed users to drop into virtual rooms and listen to live conversations on topics ranging from venture capital to cooking to conspiracy theories. It seemed to represent a new category of social media, one that solved the exact problem the pandemic had created: how to maintain spontaneous, serendipitous social interaction when physical gatherings had become impossible.

By February 2021, less than a year after the pandemic began, Clubhouse had reached a $4 billion valuation despite having only a handful of employees, no revenue model, and an invite-only system that created artificial scarcity and turned access into a status symbol. The narrative that formed around Clubhouse exemplified everything Silicon Valley wanted to believe about startups: that a small team with a simple idea could achieve massive scale almost overnight, that product-market fit would reveal itself immediately if you built something people truly wanted, and that growth, once it began, would compound exponentially without the need for traditional infrastructure or systematic operational excellence. The central tension was not whether Clubhouse could grow. Evidence of growth was everywhere, from Elon Musk hosting conversations with thousands of listeners to celebrities clamoring for access to venture capitalists, who proclaimed it the future of social media. The real question was whether the growth marked the beginning of a durable platform or merely a momentary convergence of unusual circumstances that would prove impossible to sustain once the world returned to normal.

MISTAKING CIRCUMSTANCES FOR STRATEGY

Clubhouse's strategy, to the extent one could identify a coherent framework beneath the chaos of explosive growth, centered on creating exclusivity through scarcity and then riding the resulting FOMO (fear of missing out) to achieve viral distribution without spending on user acquisition. The first critical decision was to launch invite-only, which meant that getting access required knowing someone already in the network, turning each invitation into social currency, and making the act of joining itself newsworthy enough to generate press coverage and social media buzz. The second decision emphasized live, ephemeral conversations that could not be recorded or replayed, creating an urgent incentive to participate. If you were not in the room when something interesting happened, you missed it forever, a stark contrast to platforms like YouTube or podcasts, where content remained permanently accessible.

Their third strategic pillar involved courting high-profile users early, bringing in celebrities, venture capitalists, and thought leaders who could attract audiences and create the perception that important conversations were happening only on Clubhouse. What they explicitly said no to proved revealing in retrospect: they said no to building robust content moderation systems before they were urgently needed, no to developing features that would help users discover relevant rooms beyond the main feed, no to creating tools that would enable community formation and retention, no to Android development during the crucial early period which limited them to iOS users, and no to systematic measurement of engagement depth rather than top-line growth metrics.

The framework guiding these decisions, though never articulated publicly in these terms, rested on a set of implicit assumptions. Growth would solve all problems. Viral distribution could substitute for systematic product development. Being first to capture attention in a new category would create defensibility, even without strong retention mechanics or network effects beyond simple presence. As 2021 gave way to 2022, those assumptions would prove catastrophically wrong.

WHEN THE MUSIC STOPS

The execution unfolded in two distinct phases separated by a dramatic inflection point, beginning with the extraordinary growth period from March 2020 through February 2021, when Clubhouse grew from a few thousand beta users to ten million weekly active users and reached a valuation of $4 billion on the strength of engagement metrics that suggested people were spending hours per day in rooms. During this phase, every metric increased: downloads accelerated week over week, press coverage intensified as mainstream media discovered the platform, and high-profile moments such as Elon Musk's appearance in February 2021 brought millions of new users who had been waiting for invitations. The company raised capital at increasingly aggressive valuations, hired more employees to handle growth, and became the subject of intense speculation about whether it would emerge as the next major social platform alongside Facebook, Twitter, and TikTok.

However, the second phase revealed the fragility of growth built on circumstance rather than systematic competitive advantage. It began in April 2021, when weekly active users peaked and then began a steady, inexorable decline that would ultimately see the platform lose more than 90% of its users over the following 12 months. By April 2022, weekly active users had fallen from a peak of 10 million to approximately 600,000. This collapse in engagement could not be explained solely by increased competition, though Twitter Spaces and other competitors certainly played a role. The deeper cause was that Clubhouse's growth had been driven primarily by pandemic conditions that created unusual availability and demand for virtual connection, rather than by durable product-market fit.

The obstacles they encountered multiplied as growth reversed: content moderation problems that had been manageable at small scale became existential crises as bad actors discovered they could spread misinformation without permanent records, user retention proved nearly impossible to improve without fundamental product changes that would take months to build, and the Android launch in May 2021 came too late to recapture momentum as both the pandemic circumstances and the cultural moment had shifted. The inflection point arrived not as a single dramatic moment but as a gradual realization through summer 2021 that users who had spent hours per day on the platform during lockdown were returning to in-person interactions and abandoning Clubhouse entirely rather than reducing usage—suggesting they had been substituting Clubhouse for activities they actually preferred rather than adopting it as a permanent addition to their social infrastructure.

💡 THE LESSON

Clubhouse's trajectory demonstrates the crucial distinction this chapter emphasizes between viral growth and the three forces that create sustainable competitive advantage, illustrating how a company can achieve massive user adoption without possessing velocity, momentum, or durable distribution in ways that matter for long-term success. The case validates the chapter's central argument that what appears to be overnight success almost always masks either years of prior building or, more dangerously, the absence of real foundations that will eventually cause collapse once temporary circumstances change.

Analysis using the V ∩ M ∩ D framework reveals specific failures: Clubhouse demonstrated velocity in user acquisition but not in product development. They could not ship features quickly enough to address retention problems or competitive threats, leaving them unable to adapt as circumstances changed. They achieved temporary momentum through pandemic-driven engagement but never built the systematic retention mechanisms that would survive the return to normalcy, mistaking circumstantial behavior for genuine product-market fit and failing to distinguish between users who loved the product and those who were simply filling time during an unusual period. Most critically, their distribution advantage proved entirely dependent on novelty, scarcity, and pandemic conditions rather than on network effects, viral mechanics, or other durable sources of user acquisition, meaning that once the cultural moment passed and competitors launched similar features, their growth engine completely stalled.

The memorable synthesis for founders: explosive growth that arrives without systematic building of velocity, momentum, and distribution is not the beginning of a success story but rather a dangerous illusion that can mask fundamental weaknesses, prevent necessary investment in infrastructure and capability, and create a false sense of inevitability that makes the eventual collapse both more severe and more surprising than it needed to be. Real overnight success, paradoxically, requires years of building the forces that make rapid growth sustainable once it arrives.

Where Instagram, Slack, and Stripe illustrate how compounding systems produce sudden visibility, Clubhouse shows what happens when visibility arrives first.

Key Takeaways

Stepping back, this chapter resolves into a few durable principles:

- Nearly all visible growth is preceded by long periods of obscurity, during which companies build products, iterate based on feedback, and lay the foundations that enable later scale.
- What appears as hockey-stick growth is usually the moment when accumulated advantages reach sufficient scale to make growth self-reinforcing, not the result of a sudden breakthrough.
- Narratives of overnight success persist because media coverage compresses years of effort into a single moment, social proof makes those stories feel replicable, and cultural myths glorify hero founders

and lucky breaks, often leading founders to chase appearances rather than build compounding systems.

- Growth becomes more predictable when understood as something deliberately constructed through sustained velocity and accumulated momentum, rather than something that happens unexpectedly or all at once.

The following chapters systematically examine how velocity is built within organizations, how momentum is created and sustained over time despite inevitable setbacks and challenges, and how distribution creates a lasting competitive advantage that compounds. They will challenge many of the assumptions that dominate contemporary startup thinking and replace them with frameworks that better explain how modern companies actually grow and why some succeed where most fail.

Chapter 2

Velocity Is the First Advantage

Speed of learning and iteration creates more opportunities to find what works before resources run out or markets close, making velocity the foundational advantage that enables everything else.

— *Mark Zuckerberg, Velocity Wins*

The True Nature of Speed in Startups

Velocity in physics is a vector quantity, meaning it possesses both magnitude and direction. Speed without direction is not velocity at all, merely motion without purpose. In startups, this distinction becomes absolutely critical. Velocity is not about how much activity you generate or how many hours your team logs. It is not measured in features shipped or lines of code written, or meetings attended. True velocity is about how quickly you learn what actually matters in your specific market and act decisively on that knowledge, closing the loop between hypothesis and evidence faster than competitors can.

But understanding velocity as a concept is not enough. Its real importance only becomes clear when you see what is actually at stake for a startup. Most startups move too slowly through the critical early stages of their development, not because their teams lack intelligence, work ethic, or commitment, but because they fundamentally misunderstand what speed actually means in the context of building a business. They confuse motion with progress, activity with velocity, and busyness with the kind of directed momentum that actually moves a company forward. Teams fill their calendars with meetings, their roadmaps with features, and their days with work, yet somehow find themselves no closer to product-market fit 6 months later than they were at the beginning.

The teams that win in competitive markets are not always the ones working the longest hours or maintaining the most grueling schedules. They are the ones closing the feedback loop fastest, moving through the cycle of shipping, measuring, learning, and shipping again before their competitors finish arguing about the roadmap or securing approval for their next experiment. This learning speed creates a compounding advantage that becomes increasingly difficult to overcome as the gap widens across successive iterations.

Learning Loops and Competitive Advantage

Once speed is reframed as learning rather than activity, the real engine of startup advantage becomes visible: the learning loop itself. Consider how Figma built its product in a market that seemed completely locked up by entrenched incumbents. When Dylan Field and Evan Wallace began developing a design tool that ran entirely in the browser, the prevailing view in the creative software industry was nearly unanimous: professional creative tools had to be native applications. Adobe dominated the market with desktop applications such as Photoshop and Illustrator that required years to master and even longer to develop. The barriers to entry appeared insurmountable, both technical and market-position-related.

Figma did not attempt to match Adobe feature-for-feature or compete on the terms incumbents had established. Instead, they built the simplest possible version of a multiplayer design tool that worked in a browser, shipped it to designers willing to try something new, and then watched incredibly carefully how people actually used it. Every constraint they encountered became a feature request to evaluate. Every confused user became a valuable data point on what was not working. Every point of friction in the workflow became something to address in the next release. The velocity of their learning loop meant that Figma evolved toward genuine product-market fit faster than incumbents could even recognize the threat, let alone mount an effective response.

This approach required discipline and focus that most startups lack. It would have been tempting to add features speculatively, to build what they imagined professional designers needed based on their own assumptions. Instead, they let actual usage patterns guide their development priorities, maintaining an incredibly tight loop between observation and action that allowed them to iterate based on real evidence rather than theory.

Velocity Is Not Recklessness

It is important to understand that velocity is not recklessness or carelessness about quality. Moving fast does not mean shipping fundamentally broken products or ignoring customer feedback in pursuit of arbitrary deadlines. True velocity means reducing the time between hypothesis and evidence, between idea and validation. It means making smaller bets more frequently rather than large bets infrequently. It means structuring the organization so that decisions happen at the edge where information is freshest and most relevant, rather than at the center where it gets filtered, delayed, and diluted through layers of management.

Most companies systematically lose velocity as they grow larger, and they do so for reasons that seem entirely rational in the moment. They add process to reduce risk and prevent mistakes. They add layers of management to handle increasing complexity. They add meetings to ensure alignment across growing teams. All of this is logical, but it slows learning if implemented without careful consideration of the costs. The challenge is not to avoid structure and process entirely, which would create chaos. The challenge is to design organizational structure and processes that actually accelerate learning rather than prevent it, that create clarity without rigidity, and that enable coordination without requiring constant synchronization.

Institutional Design for Speed

But fast learning does not happen by effort alone. It depends on how the company is structured to support or suppress those loops. Amazon institutionalized velocity through explicit mechanisms, such as its two-pizza team structure and its framework for distinguishing between one-way and two-way door decisions. Small teams own entire problem spaces end to end, with the authority and autonomy to make decisions without escalating everything to senior leadership. Reversible decisions, which can be undone if they prove misguided, get made quickly by the people closest to the work who have the most relevant information. Irreversible decisions, which are difficult or impossible to undo once made, receive appropriate scrutiny and deliberation. This is not about moving fast and breaking things indiscriminately. It is about moving fast on the things that can be unbroken if necessary and slowing down deliberately only where mistakes are genuinely expensive or dangerous.

This distinction between reversible and irreversible decisions is crucial because it allows organizations to maintain speed on most decisions while exercising appropriate caution on the small subset that truly requires it. Most decisions in most companies are reversible, yet they are often treated as permanent and irreversible, which creates organizational paralysis and kills velocity.

The compounding nature of velocity is perhaps its most important characteristic and the one most consistently underestimated by founders and executives. A team that learns 10% faster than its competitors will not simply beat them by 10% over time. The gap widens dramatically because each cycle of learning creates better hypotheses for the next cycle, each iteration builds on insights from the previous version, and knowledge accumulates in ways that dramatically accelerate subsequent learning. A company that ships weekly learns roughly 4 times faster than one that ships monthly, assuming they measure and learn from each release. Over the course of a year, that difference is not incremental or linear. It is categorical, representing dozens of additional learning cycles that compound into a fundamentally different understanding of the market and the customer.

The Hidden Enemies of Velocity

The enemies of velocity are not always obvious or dramatic. Sometimes velocity dies because the feature roadmap gets locked 6 months in advance, creating inflexibility that prevents the team from responding to new information. Sometimes it dies because the decision-making process requires consensus from people who do not talk to customers regularly and therefore lack current context.

Sometimes it dies because the culture punishes small failures so harshly that teams stop taking risks altogether, preferring to do nothing rather than risk doing something that might not work perfectly.

Velocity requires psychological safety within teams. Teams that fear making mistakes avoid experimenting with new approaches. They do not test bold ideas that might fail. They do not challenge fundamental assumptions about the business or the market. They optimize for not being wrong, which is a profoundly different goal than finding out what is actually right. The difference between these two orientations is the difference between stagnation and progress.

Netflix understood this dynamic deeply when it formalized its culture around the principles of freedom and responsibility. High-performing individuals had substantial autonomy to make decisions without requiring approval from lengthy chains of command. Mistakes were expected as a natural part of experimentation, not punished reflexively, as long as the learning was captured, understood, and shared across the organization. The result was an organization that could pivot from DVD rentals by mail to streaming to original content production faster than competitors who had significantly more resources but far less organizational velocity.

Clarity Enables Speed

Velocity also requires unusual clarity about direction and priorities. Teams cannot move fast if they do not know what they are moving toward or why it matters. Vision alone is not sufficient for velocity. Vision must be translated into strategy, and strategy must be translated into concrete objectives that teams can execute against without requiring constant redirection or clarification. This is where many startups fail in practice. They confuse flexibility with lack of focus, pivoting so frequently that no momentum accumulates in any particular direction. Velocity without direction is merely noise and wasted energy. The goal is not to change course every week in response to new information. The goal is to test hypotheses rapidly that move the company closer to a coherent thesis about how the business creates value and captures it sustainably.

Fast feedback loops do not happen by accident or through good intentions. They are deliberately designed into how the company operates. Companies with high velocity instrument their products carefully to see what users actually do, not just what they say they want or need. They run experiments constantly, sometimes dozens at a time. They ship features behind feature flags so they can test new functionality in production with real users without risking a bad experience for everyone. They make data accessible to everyone in the organization, not locked away in dashboards that only executives can see, because widespread access to data enables better decisions at every level.

Velocity represents the first advantage in building a startup because it fundamentally determines how quickly you find product-market fit. It determines how fast you can adapt when market conditions shift or competitors make moves. It determines whether you learn from competitors or they learn from you, whether you set the pace or respond to it. Every other advantage in business can eventually be purchased with sufficient capital or copied with sufficient effort. Velocity is structural rather than tactical. It lives in how a company makes decisions, how teams are organized and empowered, how learning is prioritized and disseminated, and how feedback loops are constructed and maintained.

The startups that will dominate their markets over the next decade are being built right now by teams that ship, learn, and adapt faster than everyone else in their space. They are not waiting for perfect information before acting. They are creating information through action, through experimentation, through putting things into the world and watching what happens. They are not endlessly debating what might work in conference rooms. They are testing hypotheses in the market to find out what actually works in practice.

Velocity is not the only thing that matters in building a successful company, but it is the foundational capability that makes everything else possible. Without velocity, even the best ideas arrive too late to matter. Without velocity, momentum cannot be built. Without velocity, distribution advantages erode. Speed of learning and execution is the starting point from which everything else flows.

 *Case Study - Monzo*

Building a Bank at Startup Speed

To see what happens when these principles are applied under extreme real-world constraints, consider Monzo. In 2015, when Tom Blomfield and his co-founders began the arduous process of obtaining a banking license in the United Kingdom, the prevailing wisdom in financial services held that banking and velocity were fundamentally incompatible concepts that could not coexist within a single organization. Traditional banks moved slowly, not because of incompetence or lack of ambition, but because the industry's regulatory framework, built over centuries of financial crises and consumer protection failures, essentially mandated caution over speed, extensive testing over rapid iteration, and institutional risk management over entrepreneurial experimentation.

The timeline for launching a new bank typically spanned 3 to 5 years from initial concept to serving customers, requiring not only 18 months to obtain regulatory approval but also tens of millions of pounds in capital reserves, legacy banking infrastructure that had been proven over decades, and a corporate culture oriented toward preventing problems rather than moving fast and breaking things. Monzo's founding team believed they could challenge this orthodoxy by building a bank that operated with the velocity of a software startup while simultaneously building the momentum of genuine customer love and the distribution advantages of viral growth, arguing that the three-forces framework could apply even in the most regulated, risk-averse industry imaginable.

The stakes extended beyond commercial success or failure; if Monzo moved too fast and encountered a security breach, regulatory violation, or operational failure that put customer deposits at risk, they would not get a second chance to rebuild trust, and their failure would likely set back the entire challenger bank movement by years. The central tension revolved around whether it was possible to build financial infrastructure with startup velocity, whether customers would trust a bank that did not have marble lobbies and century-old brand heritage, and whether regulators would allow a company that shipped code weekly to hold banking licenses that gave them access to the payments system and deposit insurance, questions that would not be answered theoretically but only through the difficult process of actually building the thing.

THE THREE FORCES AS A DELIBERATE SYSTEM

Monzo's strategic framework rested on the insight that the three forces, velocity, momentum, and distribution, did not need to be built sequentially but could instead be developed in parallel through careful prioritization and willingness to make counterintuitive trade-offs that traditional banks would never accept. The first critical decision was to launch initially as a prepaid card rather than a full bank. This allowed them to get a product into customers' hands within months rather than years while they navigated the longer banking license process. It laid the foundation for building momentum and distribution, even before they had velocity in the regulatory domain. This decision proved controversial within the founding team because prepaid cards carried stigma in the UK market as products for people who could not qualify for real bank accounts. But Blomfield argued that learning velocity mattered more than brand positioning in the early days, and that real users with real money at stake would provide infinitely more valuable feedback than focus groups or theoretical product development.

The second strategic pillar focused on building community before building features. The team invested heavily in customer support, transparency, and user forums, transforming early adopters into evangelists who would drive distribution through word-of-mouth and social media advocacy. They made the radical decision: hiring customer support representatives who could make real decisions rather than following scripts, publishing internal metrics and challenges publicly through their blog and social media, and treating the community forum as a product feedback mechanism that directly influenced the product roadmap. Though these choices cost money and management attention, they created momentum through genuine customer advocacy rather than paid marketing.

Their third strategic bet involved embracing mobile-first architecture not as a feature but as a constraint that would force better design decisions. They explicitly chose not to build desktop banking, physical branches, or legacy system compatibility in ways that would slow their development velocity. What they said no to proved as important as what they said yes to: no to launching in multiple countries simultaneously despite investor pressure for faster growth, no to building every feature traditional banks offered just to achieve feature parity, no to traditional marketing spending in favor of investing in product velocity and customer experience, no to hiring banking industry veterans into senior roles when they could instead hire technologists who understood velocity, and no to quarterly planning cycles in favor of continuous deployment and weekly iterations.

The framework guiding these decisions held that the three forces created compounding advantages when built together. Velocity in product development created better customer experiences, which built momentum through retention and advocacy. This momentum enabled distribution without paid marketing, which in turn attracted more users whose feedback accelerated velocity. That virtuous cycle, once established, would prove defensible against both traditional banks, who could not match their velocity, and other startups, who might build fast but could not build the regulatory moats and operational complexity that came with being a real bank.

WHEN THEORY MEETS REGULATED REALITY

Monzo's execution unfolded across four distinct phases that demonstrated how the three forces compounded over time. It began with the prepaid card launch in 2015, when Monzo released its coral-colored debit cards to a small group of beta users. They focused obsessively on building velocity in their development process while simultaneously laying the foundations for the community that would later drive momentum.

During these 18 months before receiving their full banking license, they shipped product updates weekly. They responded to customer support queries within minutes rather than days. They also built a community forum that attracted thousands of engaged users who provided detailed feedback and became unpaid advocates for the product. This established patterns of velocity and momentum-building that would characterize their approach for years to come.

The second phase began in April 2017, when they received their full banking license and could finally offer standard bank accounts with deposit protection. This marked an inflection point at which their accumulated velocity and momentum could suddenly access a much larger distribution. They were no longer limited to the prepaid card market. Within 12 months of receiving the license, they grew from 100,000 prepaid card users to more than 1 million full current account customers. This growth was powered not by advertising spending but by word-of-mouth distribution from existing customers and the distinctive coral card, which became a visible signal in coffee shops and restaurants across London.

The third phase, spanning 2018 through 2020, tested whether their model could scale beyond early adopters to mainstream customers. This required building operational infrastructure and compliance systems capable of handling millions of transactions daily while maintaining the velocity that had defined their early success. They encountered significant obstacles during this period. A major outage in July 2019 left customers unable to access their accounts for an entire day, forcing a reckoning with their technical infrastructure and development practices. Regulatory scrutiny around their financial crime controls required massive investment in compliance systems. There was also the constant tension between maintaining startup velocity and building the operational excellence required of an institution holding billions of pounds in customer deposits.

The inflection point that validated their three-forces approach arrived during the COVID pandemic in 2020. Traditional banks struggled to adapt their services to lockdown conditions. Meanwhile, Monzo's mobile-first architecture and rapid development velocity allowed them to ship new features weekly to address changing customer needs. This enabled them to gain market share even as the economic crisis put pressure on their business model. By 2022, they had grown to more than five million customers and achieved profitability for the first time. They also demonstrated that the three forces framework could work even in highly regulated industries that conventional wisdom said required slow, cautious approaches, though not without near-death experiences and painful lessons about when velocity needed to slow down to build proper foundations.

💡 THE LESSON

Monzo's journey validates this chapter's framework by demonstrating how velocity, momentum, and distribution create compounding advantages when built deliberately and in parallel rather than sequentially. It also illustrates the crucial insight that the three forces do not eliminate the need for operational excellence, regulatory compliance, or sound unit economics. Instead, they accelerate the path to discovering what needs to be built and create competitive advantages that make the difficult work of building infrastructure worthwhile.

Analyzing through the V ∩ M ∩ D lens reveals how each force multiplied the others. Their velocity in shipping product improvements created better customer experiences, which built momentum through satisfaction and retention. This enabled word-of-mouth distribution that brought in more customers. Customers' feedback and usage patterns enabled even faster velocity in identifying and solving problems. The result was a flywheel that traditional banks could not match because they lacked velocity. Challenger banks could not match it either because they lacked the momentum and distribution that came from genuinely superior product experience.

The case also demonstrates the framework's applicability beyond software startups. Even in banking, which is perhaps the most regulated, trust-dependent, infrastructure-heavy industry imaginable, the three forces create sustainable competitive advantage if founders can navigate the apparent contradiction between startup velocity and institutional responsibility.

Most critically for founders reading this chapter, Monzo's experience illustrates that building all three forces simultaneously requires explicit trade-offs and a willingness to say no to opportunities that would compromise the framework. They said no to faster geographic expansion that would have diluted their velocity. They said no to feature bloat that would have compromised product clarity and momentum. They said no to paid marketing that would have undermined their distribution model built on genuine advocacy. And they said yes to the harder path: building a bank that operated fundamentally differently from incumbents, rather than simply offering a slightly better user interface on top of traditional banking infrastructure.

The memorable synthesis: the three forces framework does not make hard things easy. But it does make hard things winnable by creating compounding advantages that accumulate over time. Initial disadvantages in resources, brand recognition, and market position become irrelevant as velocity, momentum, and distribution combine to create growth that appears effortless from the outside. In reality, it represents years of deliberate systems-building that made the seemingly overnight success both possible and sustainable.

Key Takeaways

Taken together, the chapter clarifies what velocity means in practice:

- Velocity is meaningful progress, not reckless speed. True velocity measures the rate of learning and iteration that advances objectives that matter most for the business, enabling faster discovery of product-market fit, customer needs, and effective distribution strategies.

- Velocity depends on structure and architecture. Small teams with minimal coordination overhead and technical systems designed for rapid iteration can sustain meaningful progress without accumulating debt or bottlenecks that slow development.
- Sustained velocity compounds advantage. Teams that maintain even marginally higher velocity over time accumulate dramatically more learning, iteration, and progress, creating a long-term compounding effect that competitors struggle to match.

Monzo, Figma, Amazon, and Netflix all demonstrate that velocity is not about working harder; it is about designing systems, culture, and processes that accelerate learning. The companies that dominate tomorrow are already building the structures today to move, learn, and adapt faster than anyone else.

For founders, velocity is the ultimate leverage; the multiplier that turns limited resources into an outsized advantage. But velocity alone is not enough. Its true power is realized when it is sustained and focused, creating patterns of progress that compound over time. The next challenge is to take this initial speed and turn it into momentum: the force that carries every action forward and makes each subsequent step more impactful than the last.

In the following chapter, we will explore how momentum is built deliberately and why it is the natural evolution of velocity into lasting advantage.

Chapter 3

Momentum Is Built, Not Found

When I look over the good-to-great transformations, the one word that keeps coming to mind is consistency… Each piece of the system reinforces the other parts of the system to form an integrated whole that is much more powerful than the sum of the parts.

— *Jim Collins, Good to Great*

The Difference Between Noise and Progress

Velocity opens the door to progress and possibility. Momentum carries it forward, increasing in magnitude. While velocity is about the rate of movement and learning, momentum is about the persistence and compounding nature of that movement over time. Momentum is the sense that a business is genuinely working at a fundamental level: growth is not fragile or dependent on constant intervention, but rather has its own internal logic and energy that carries it forward.

Momentum represents the compounding effect of repeated progress in the same general direction. It is the point in a startup's development at which growth feels inevitable rather than precarious, where each new customer or user makes the next one easier to acquire rather than harder, and where the business begins to pull the founders and team forward rather than requiring them to push constantly just to maintain position. It emerges when velocity is sustained over time and directed toward building specific advantages that make each subsequent action more effective than the previous one. It is what investors seek to identify when they discuss traction, and what founders feel viscerally when the business begins generating its own energy rather than consuming it.

Momentum is also perhaps the most misunderstood and misidentified force in startups. Founders often believe they have momentum when they do not, mistaking temporary spikes or isolated successes for sustained trends. They see a sudden increase in signups after a Product Hunt launch and interpret it as momentum rather than a one-time event. They close a significant customer and assume the sales pipeline will naturally fill with similar opportunities. They receive coverage in a major publication and believe the market has validated their approach. All of these can be encouraging signals, but none of them constitute proof of genuine momentum.

The Persistence Test

To understand how momentum differs from mere activity, we must examine its persistence over time and the mechanisms that allow it to compound. Real momentum persists beyond the immediate catalyst that created it. It does not require constant intervention or repeated energy injections to sustain itself. It builds on itself through internal mechanisms that make each successive unit of growth easier than the last. Each new customer acquired makes the next customer easier to acquire, whether through word-of-mouth, improved unit economics that enable more aggressive customer acquisition, or network effects that increase the product's value. Each feature shipped increases the product's value to existing users and its appeal to potential users. Each piece of content published builds authority and visibility, thereby attracting the next wave of audience attention. Momentum is not a moment in time or a single metric spike. It is a trend that maintains its trajectory through its own internal dynamics.

The fundamental problem is that most startups experience significant volatility rather than genuine momentum in their early stages. They have a strong month, followed by a flat or even declining month. They acquire users in concentrated bursts that fade quickly rather than sustaining or accelerating. They ship features that create temporary spikes in engagement but do not meaningfully change retention curves or expand usage over time. This pattern is not momentum. This is noise, random variation around a mean that may or may not be trending upward over longer time horizons.

Noise looks deceptively like progress when you zoom in to short time frames. It feels productive because things are happening, numbers are changing, and there is activity to report. But when you zoom out to longer time scales, there is no consistent trajectory. The line does not point reliably up and to the right. Instead, it jumps around unpredictably, responding to individual events and initiatives rather than showing the signature of a system that is genuinely working. Companies that mistake noise for momentum make systematically bad decisions. They double down on tactics that produced one-time results, which cannot be replicated. They over-index on anecdotal feedback that is not representative. They chase the subjective feeling of activity and motion rather than confronting the objective reality of whether growth is compounding over time.

Building Through Consistency

Persistence alone is not enough; sustained progress requires clarity and consistent focus on the core problem the company is solving. This does not mean consistency in tactics, which may need to evolve as the market changes and the company learns. It means consistency in direction, in the fundamental problem being solved, in the value proposition being refined, and in the customer segment being served. Airbnb did not build momentum by trying every possible approach to marketplaces or travel. They built it by repeatedly solving the same fundamental problem with increasing sophistication: making strangers trust one another enough to share homes. Every feature they added, every policy they implemented, every piece of communication they crafted reinforced that central goal. The marketplace grew not because of a single viral mechanism or clever hack, but because each incremental improvement made the platform more trustworthy, thereby increasing hosts' willingness to list their properties and guests' willingness to book unfamiliar accommodations.

This kind of consistency requires clarity about strategy and remarkable discipline in execution. It is far easier to pursue new opportunities as they arise, to pivot frequently when growth slows, and to experiment with different value propositions for different customer segments. Consistency does not mean rigidity or inability to adapt. Markets change constantly. Customer needs evolve in response to new alternatives. Competitors adapt and force strategic responses. The critical question is whether your adjustments represent refinements of a clear, stable strategy or evidence that you lack a coherent strategy and are searching for one reactively. Companies with genuine momentum know what they are building and why it matters. They might change how they execute specific tactics or which features they prioritize, but they do not fundamentally alter their quarterly thesis on value creation.

The Fragility of Early Momentum

Even with a clear focus, early momentum is delicate and can be lost without careful discipline. A startup can simultaneously be

3 weeks away from a significant breakthrough and 3 weeks away from running out of runway with no clear path to additional capital. The difference between these outcomes is often not visible within the company, where activity and effort appear constant regardless of whether they generate momentum or merely create motion. This inherent fragility is why discipline is so important during the phase when momentum is building but not yet stable. Companies that preserve and amplify early momentum are those that protect what is demonstrably working while carefully testing what might work better, never killing the engines that are running while trying to build new ones.

One of the most common and destructive ways startups accidentally kill early momentum is by scaling prematurely. They observe initial traction in a specific channel or with a particular customer segment and immediately assume it is time to pour fuel on the fire through aggressive expansion. They hire rapidly across multiple functions. They expand into new marketing channels before fully understanding what made the initial channel work. They add features targeting customer segments they have not properly validated. They internationalize before dominating their initial market. The growth they confidently expect does not materialize at the required rate to justify the increased burn, and they suddenly spend far more cash with no corresponding increase in revenue or a sustainable growth rate. The fragile momentum they thought they had evaporated under the weight of premature organizational scale and strategic diffusion.

Scaling Versus Growing

It is crucial to understand that scaling is fundamentally different from growth, and conflating the two leads to systematic strategic errors. Growth occurs when you discover something that works and do more of it, thereby expanding the volume of activity within a proven model. Scaling is the process of building systems and infrastructure to execute a proven model without requiring proportional increases in human attention or intervention. Companies that attempt to scale before they have real momentum are building elaborate infrastructure for a business model they have not yet validated. They are optimizing for a future that may never arrive, investing heavily in systems before understanding whether the underlying model actually works at scale.

Momentum also demands sharp focus rather than broad diffusion of effort. Startups that try to serve everyone simultaneously serve no one particularly well. They dilute their marketing message, trying to appeal to multiple distinct audiences. They confuse their product direction by trying to solve different problems for different segments. They spread their limited resources so thin that nothing receives the sustained attention required to truly compound. The companies that build lasting momentum are often maniacally focused on a specific customer with a specific problem during their early phases. They become the obvious, dominant choice for that narrow segment before attempting to expand into adjacent markets or customer types.

Stripe exemplifies this approach to building momentum through focus. They started with developers, but not developers generally. They focused specifically on developers seeking to accept online payments without the complexity of legacy financial infrastructure. They made their API so elegant and their integration so straightforward that developers actively advocated for Stripe inside their companies, creating bottom-up adoption that traditional enterprise sales approaches could not match. That developer advocacy became the engine of momentum. Only after they had achieved clear dominance with that initial segment did they methodically expand into adjacent markets, always building on the foundation of what they had already proven. They did not try to become a comprehensive payment processor for every type of business on day one. They became the best option for a specific group and leveraged momentum to enter broader markets from that position of strength.

Measuring What Matters

Momentum becomes visible through specific metrics that matter for your particular business model, though these metrics are often lagging indicators that tell you whether you had momentum rather than whether you currently have it. For a SaaS company, genuine momentum shows up in net revenue retention, the percentage of revenue from existing customers that you retain and expand over time. In marketplaces, it appears in repeat-transaction rates and the percentage of users who make multiple purchases. In a consumer application, this manifests as weekly active users who persist for months and gradually increase their usage. These are lagging indicators precisely because they measure outcomes over extended time periods, but they are reliable in ways that vanity metrics are not. They do not lie or mislead the way that top-line signup numbers or social media followers can.

The reason momentum is so powerful once established is that it fundamentally changes the psychology and dynamics of the entire business. When a company has genuine momentum, recruiting suddenly becomes easier because talented people want to join companies that are clearly winning. Customers become more forgiving of rough edges and gaps in functionality because they can see the trajectory of improvement. Investors pay attention without requiring extensive outreach. Press coverage happens organically because journalists are looking for growth stories. Momentum creates a halo effect that makes every subsequent action more effective and every investment more productive than it would be without that underlying energy.

The Limits of Narrative

However, momentum cannot be manufactured through narrative alone, though many founders try this approach precisely. Press releases announcing partnerships or milestones do not create momentum. Elaborate launch events do not create momentum. Expensive marketing campaigns do not create momentum if the underlying business is not working. Momentum emerges from a business that is genuinely working at a fundamental level, where the unit economics are sound and improving, where customers keep coming back and expanding their usage, and where the product delivers sufficient value that people actively choose it over alternatives. No amount of narrative or marketing sophistication can substitute for these underlying fundamentals.

Founders who truly understand momentum protect it with unusual vigilance and discipline. They do not take random meetings that distract from core priorities. They do not pursue shiny opportunities that divert attention from what is working. They do not allow organizational distractions to derail the core business. They recognize that momentum is perhaps the most valuable asset they possess, and once lost, it is extraordinarily difficult to rebuild. The market forgives almost anything in a company with momentum. The market is merciless toward companies that lose momentum and struggle to regain it.

Momentum ultimately represents what separates projects from businesses, experiments from companies, and motion from genuine progress. A project is something you push constantly just to maintain position. A business is something that pulls itself and you forward. When you have built genuine momentum, the market starts to pull your product forward through its own dynamics. That transition from pushing to being pulled is the fundamental transformation every startup is attempting to achieve. Velocity gets you to that inflection point. Momentum sustains you beyond it. But only if you can recognize the difference between real momentum and the comforting illusion of activity, and only if you refuse to confuse motion with meaningful progress toward your ultimate goals.

🔍 *Case Study - Jumia*

When Expansion Confuses Motion with Momentum

Jumia's experience shows how expansion can create the illusion of momentum while masking underlying weaknesses. In 2012, when Rocket Internet launched Jumia as the "Amazon of Africa" with the explicit strategy of rapidly capturing e-commerce market share across the continent before local competitors could establish themselves, the playbook seemed straightforward: replicate successful Western business models in emerging markets with speed and capital intensity that would create insurmountable first-mover advantages. The opportunity appeared massive, a continent of 1.3 billion people with rapidly growing internet penetration, rising middle-class consumption, and virtually no organized e-commerce infrastructure.

Jumia launched with extraordinary ambition, expanding from Nigeria to 14 African countries within 5 years, building logistics networks where none existed, recruiting thousands of employees, and spending heavily on customer acquisition to establish brand recognition. By 2019, just 7 years after launch, Jumia became the first African startup to list on the New York Stock Exchange with an opening market capitalization exceeding $3.5 billion, seemingly validating the blitzscaling approach and suggesting that rapid geographic expansion could create the momentum necessary to dominate African e-commerce.

Yet this narrative conflated geographic expansion with momentum-building, mistaking presence across multiple markets for compounding advantages within those markets, and conflating customer-acquisition spend with genuine retention that would create self-sustaining growth.

EXPENSIVE MOTION

Jumia's execution revealed the distinction between expansion and momentum, as evidenced by patterns that became increasingly problematic as it scaled. The first critical issue involved customer-acquisition economics that did not improve with scale: they spent heavily on subsidies, advertising, and promotions to attract customers, but those customers did not return at rates sufficient to cover acquisition costs, resulting in high Customer Acquisition Cost (CAC) without corresponding lifetime value.

The metric that exposed this problem was net revenue retention, the percentage of revenue from existing customers that continued or grew over time, which remained stubbornly low as they discovered that customers acquired through discounts were inherently price-sensitive and would switch to competitors once subsidies ended.

The second strategic misstep centered on treating geographic expansion as momentum building when it actually multiplied complexity without creating advantages: operating in 14 countries meant navigating 14 different regulatory environments, building 14 separate logistics networks, managing 14 different payment infrastructures, but these expansions did not create network effects or economies of scale because e-commerce is fundamentally local in terms of logistics, inventory, and customer behavior.

What they should have built but did not was retention momentum in their initial markets before expanding; the compounding advantages that come from customers returning without prompting, from word-of-mouth reducing acquisition costs, from operational learning improving unit economics, and from merchant relationships creating supply advantages. The third failure involved mistaking activity for progress: they had velocity in terms of expansion speed and marketing spend, and they had distribution in terms of geographic presence, but they lacked momentum because nothing they were building compounded over time to make future growth easier or cheaper than past growth.

SCALE WITHOUT STRENGTH

The company's evolution can be understood in three distinct phases, each revealing a critical insight: scale without sustained momentum ultimately weakens, rather than strengthens, a business. The first phase, 2012 through 2019, focused on rapid expansion and achieving a NYSE listing, which, on the surface, appeared successful: they processed transactions across 14 countries, achieved hundreds of millions in Gross Merchandise Value (GMV), built a recognizable brand, and attracted investment from prominent institutional investors. Yet beneath the growth metrics, the fundamentals revealed the absence of momentum: customer acquisition costs remained high, repeat purchase rates remained low, contribution margins per order remained negative, and geographic expansion only compounded these problems.

The second phase began immediately after their April 2019 NYSE debut when public market scrutiny exposed what private market investors had overlooked: short-seller reports alleging inflated metrics, forensic analysis revealing a substantial portion of orders were never delivered or fraudulent, and analyst reports showing that even aggressive growth projections could not generate positive economics given their retention and margin challenges. The stock, which opened at around $14.50 per share, began a steady decline as markets reassessed whether they were building sustainable businesses or simply burning capital to acquire temporary market share.

The third phase, 2020 through 2023, represented painful contraction as reality imposed discipline: they retreated from multiple countries to focus on core markets, laid off substantial workforce to reduce losses, slashed marketing spend which immediately caused growth rates to plummet, and the stock declined to under $3 per share by 2023, more than 80 percent below IPO price, as markets recognized that they had built expensive motion without genuine momentum.

💡 THE LESSON

Jumia's struggles validate this chapter's central argument that momentum must be built through compounding advantages rather than achieved through expansion or purchased through customer-acquisition spend. Analyzing their trajectory reveals how all three forces were present in surface form but missing in substance: they had velocity in terms of expansion speed but not in terms of organizational learning; they had distribution in terms of geographic presence but not in terms of efficient customer acquisition; and they completely lacked momentum because nothing they built made future growth easier or cheaper than past growth.

The case demonstrates that expansion can create the illusion of momentum, covering more geography, acquiring more customers, and generating more revenue. But if the underlying unit economics do not work and customers do not return organically, then scale amplifies losses rather than creating advantages.

The memorable synthesis: Jumia expanded to 14 African countries and achieved a New York Stock Exchange listing, seemingly building the "Amazon of Africa," but actually demonstrated that geographic expansion without retention momentum creates expensive motion rather than sustainable business, and that you cannot find momentum through expansion or buy it through customer acquisition spending. You must build it through compounding advantages that make each customer cheaper to acquire and more valuable to retain than the last.

Most critically for founders, Jumia illustrates that momentum in competitive markets requires solving retention before scaling acquisition, building genuine advantages that compound rather than simply moving fast. It requires honestly assessing whether growth is becoming easier over time or whether it requires a constant infusion of capital to sustain it.

Key Takeaways

Momentum is not a moment; it is a condition created over time.

- Momentum is a gradual accumulation of compounding advantages across product, market position, and operations. When multiple advantages reinforce each other, they create feedback loops that accelerate growth from linear to exponential.
- Building momentum requires strategic focus on specific advantages rather than spreading resources across too many opportunities, which prevents going deep enough to create defensibility.
- Momentum is fragile and must be actively sustained. It can be lost through distraction, premature scaling, or abandoning advantages too early, and requires continuously identifying and building the next set of advantages before current ones lose effectiveness.

The next step is to look more closely at what drives the compounding advantages that make momentum real, in the next chapter.

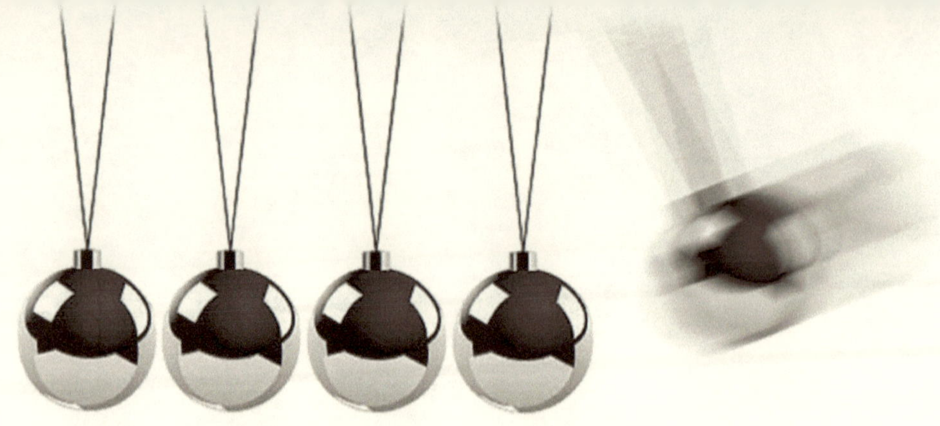

Chapter 4

Product Does Not Win Alone

The products that drive sustainable growth are not those that merely solve problems but those that become progressively more valuable to customers over time through data, habits, and integration into workflows.

— Aakash Gupta, Product Growth

The Dangerous Myth of Product Supremacy

The belief that the best product inevitably wins in the market is one of the most persistent and damaging myths in the startup ecosystem. This is one of the hardest truths for founders to internalize, particularly for those from engineering or product backgrounds, where the primacy of technical excellence often seems self-evident.

The mythology runs deep through Silicon Valley culture, reinforced by survivorship bias and simplified narratives about successful companies that emphasize their product innovations while downplaying or ignoring the distribution and go-to-market advantages that often mattered more.

History provides countless examples of technically superior products losing decisively to inferior alternatives. For example, Betamax offered demonstrably better video quality than VHS, yet lost the format war because VHS had better distribution through rental stores and longer recording times that consumers valued more than marginal quality improvements. Google+ launched with more sophisticated features and stronger privacy controls than Facebook at the time. Yet, they failed because Facebook had network effects and switching costs that rendered those features largely irrelevant. Quibi had vastly higher production values and more recognizable talent than TikTok, yet collapsed within months, even as TikTok reached billions of users, because high production value mattered far less than the distribution mechanisms and engagement loops that TikTok had built.

In each case and in countless others, the better product failed while the product with better distribution won decisively, demonstrating that distribution and engagement loops often outweigh product quality.

Necessary But Not Sufficient

A great product is necessary but not sufficient for building a successful business. Product excellence is table stakes in competitive markets; it is the baseline requirement to be considered seriously. It gets you into the game and permits you to compete. But winning the game requires a distribution strategy, go-to-market excellence, appropriate timing, network effects, and often elements of luck that cannot be fully controlled. Founders who believe that product quality alone will carry them to success are setting themselves up for a painful education in market realities.

The mythology of product-first thinking is particularly pervasive in technology circles. "Build something people want" has become a mantra, suggesting that if you create sufficient value, customers will somehow find you. This may have been approximately true during the early internet era when competition was relatively sparse, discovery mechanisms were more open, and building any reasonable product gave you visibility in an uncrowded landscape. It is emphatically not true now.

The current problem is not building something good, though that remains difficult. The problem is getting anyone to notice your good product in a world where thousands of well-executed products launch every month, where attention is scarce and expensive, and where customers are overwhelmed by alternatives.

Designing Products That Win Markets

Product quality does matter enormously, but not in the way most founders instinctively think. The goal is not to build the objectively best product based on an abstract set of technical criteria. The goal is to build the product that wins in the specific market you are competing in, which is a fundamentally different design problem.

A winning product has characteristics that extend well beyond features, performance, and polish. Winning products are built explicitly to grow. They contain mechanisms that encourage sharing, repeated use, habitual engagement, and expansion within accounts or networks. They reduce friction not only in the core experience but also in all secondary actions that drive growth, such as inviting teammates, sharing outputs, or integrating with other tools in the user's workflow.

Slack exemplifies this principle of designing growth directly into the product architecture. The collaboration tool performs significantly better when more team members use it, creating natural incentives for existing users to invite colleagues. Public channels increase visibility into work that might otherwise occur in siloed email threads, thereby demonstrating value to team members who have not yet fully adopted the platform. Integrations with other tools in the workflow make Slack stickier over time as it becomes the central communication hub.

None of these is an accidental product decision. They are deliberate design choices that make the product more valuable as it spreads and create natural, organic growth mechanisms that do not depend primarily on paid acquisition.

Retention as Foundation

While designing products to grow and engage users is critical, all these mechanisms are meaningless if customers do not stick around. Retention is the single most important measure of whether a product is truly working and capable of generating compounding value. A product that users abandon after a single attempt is not a product, regardless of how well-designed the initial experience is.

Retention is the foundation on which all sustainable growth is built. Without retention, customer acquisition becomes a perpetually leaking bucket, in which every dollar spent acquiring users is wasted because those users do not remain long enough to generate sufficient lifetime value. The unit economics become impossible. Growth becomes unsustainable without continuous injections of capital.

Products that retain users well do so because they deliver genuine, sustained value that integrates into users' workflows or lives. They solve real problems frequently enough that users develop habits around them. They become part of the user's routine rather than novelties to try once and forget. Notion grew primarily through retention and word-of-mouth rather than aggressive marketing because people who adopted it found it genuinely useful for organizing their work and lives. They continued using it, expanded its use, and informed others about it. That retention created the foundation for sustainable growth at reasonable unit economics.

The mistake many product teams make is to optimize exclusively for activation and initial engagement, while giving insufficient attention to longer-term retention and habit formation. They design elaborate onboarding flows that convert visitors into users, but do not deliver sustained value that converts users into retained, habitual customers. They celebrate sign-up metrics and first-time usage without carefully tracking whether those users return daily, weekly, or ever again. This creates a false sense of progress, where top-line numbers look encouraging, but underlying cohort retention shows the product is not actually working.

Speed of Value Delivery

Retention sets the foundation, but even a product that retains users can falter if it takes too long to deliver value. How quickly customers experience the product's core promise directly influences whether they stick, share, and create compounding growth. Products that require extensive setup or long learning curves before users experience core value have much higher abandonment rates. Time to value is a critical product metric that teams should obsess over as much as any feature roadmap.

Figma recognized this principle and focused intensely on reducing friction in the initial experience. A designer could click a link, immediately start designing in the browser without downloading or installing anything, and invite collaborators to the same file with a simple link. This near-instant time-to-value was a competitive advantage at least as important as their feature set.

Dropbox similarly recognized that time-to-value determined adoption. Their core magic was that installing Dropbox and dropping files into a folder made those files immediately accessible everywhere, with no configuration required. The product delivered its core promise within minutes of installation, creating an immediate "aha moment" that drove retention and word-of-mouth.

Product as Growth Strategy

The reality that a product alone does not win should not be misinterpreted as suggesting that a product does not matter or that distribution can overcome fundamental product weakness. The correct interpretation is that product and distribution must be thought about together as an integrated system rather than as separate domains. Product decisions are distribution decisions. The distribution strategy should inform product strategy. The best companies think about this integration from the beginning rather than building a product in isolation and then trying to figure out how to distribute it later.

Superhuman, the email client, illustrates this. They designed their product with pricing and positioning as core product decisions from the beginning. The high price point was not a monetization afterthought but a deliberate product and brand choice that positioned the application as a premium tool for professionals who use email. The invite-only launch mechanism created exclusivity and status, accelerating word-of-mouth. The onboarding process included a white-glove setup call that simultaneously educated users and reinforced the premium positioning. These were product decisions that were simultaneously distribution and brand decisions, showing how the best companies integrate these considerations from the beginning.

When Good Products Fail

Even when products are designed for growth and integrated with strategy, success is not guaranteed. Understanding the limits of product alone, and why good products can fail, reinforces the need to think beyond features and polish.

Products can be genuinely good, solving real problems in elegant ways, yet still fail commercially for reasons unrelated to product quality. They fail because the market is not ready for the solution. They fail because the distribution channels available to them are too expensive or inefficient for their price point and business model. They fail because competitors have network effects or ecosystem advantages that make switching difficult, regardless of product superiority. They fail because the team cannot execute a go-to-market strategy effectively, even when the product is sound.

Understanding this reality requires unusual humility from founders who are naturally and appropriately proud of what they have built. It requires recognizing that building a great product is perhaps 20 to 30 percent of what it takes to build a great business, not the 80 to 90 percent that product-focused founders often assume. The remaining 70 to 80 percent is distribution, positioning, pricing, go-to-market execution, and all the unglamorous work of actually getting the product into the hands of customers who will pay for it and keep using it.

The startups that will dominate their markets are those that achieve excellence in both product and distribution, understanding that these are not separate challenges but deeply interconnected parts of a single system. They build products designed from the beginning to attract and retain users. They think about distribution not as an afterthought but as a core part of their product strategy. They recognize that in competitive markets, distribution advantages compound just as powerfully as product advantages, and often more so.

Product excellence remains essential. Without it, nothing else matters because users will churn no matter how good your distribution is. But product excellence is the foundation, not the complete building.

The companies that win are those that build excellent products and then do everything else required to win markets, recognizing that the best product is only the beginning of the journey toward building a lasting business.

🔍 *Case Study - Faire*

When Exceptional Product Needs Distribution and Positioning to Scale

In 2017, when Max Rhodes, Marcelo Cortes, Daniele Perito, and Jeffrey Kolovson launched Faire as a wholesale marketplace connecting independent retailers with emerging brands, they entered a market where exceptional product quality alone had never been sufficient for marketplace success. The wholesale industry represented a $6 trillion global market characterized by deeply entrenched inefficiencies: brands struggled to reach independent retailers beyond major trade shows, retailers could not efficiently discover new products that would differentiate their stores, minimum order quantities prevented experimentation, payment terms created cash flow problems for small businesses, and returns processes made trying new brands financially risky.

Faire's founding team, coming from backgrounds at Square where they had built successful products, understood that solving these problems with elegant software would create an exceptional product experience, and they did, building a marketplace with superior search and discovery, streamlined ordering, integrated payments, and data-driven recommendations that made wholesale buying dramatically easier than legacy processes. Yet they also recognized what many product-focused founders miss: that an exceptional product creates a necessary but insufficient condition for marketplace success, and that scaling from initial traction to market leadership requires intentionally building distribution channels and positioning strategy that work in concert with product quality.

BEYOND PRODUCT EXCELLENCE

Faire's approach demonstrated how product, distribution, and positioning must develop as an interconnected system rather than sequential priorities. The first strategic insight was to design product features specifically for retention and viral growth rather than simply solving immediate user problems. Their net-30 payment terms, which allowed retailers to try products and sell them before paying suppliers, removed the cash flow risk that had historically prevented independent stores from experimenting with new brands. This was not just a convenient feature but a retention mechanism that made it financially safer to try Faire than traditional wholesale.

Their free returns policy on opening orders similarly transformed product feature into a growth lever by eliminating downside risk for retailers trying new suppliers, creating economic incentive for experimentation that drove both initial adoption and subsequent repeat behavior. These features produced remarkable retention metrics: net revenue retention exceeded 130%, meaning existing retailers were spending 30% more each year than the previous year, demonstrating that product design had successfully created compounding value that increased over time rather than simply solving a one-time problem.

The second strategic pillar focused on building distribution to reach independent retailers who were not actively seeking wholesale solutions. While inbound marketing, like content, SEO, and word-of-mouth, worked for attracting retailers already frustrated with existing wholesale processes, Faire recognized that winning market share required proactive outreach to retailers who had adapted to legacy inefficiencies and were not actively seeking alternatives.

They built an inside sales team that could educate retailers about marketplace benefits, explain how net-30 terms and free returns eliminated traditional risks, and onboard stores that would never have discovered Faire through passive channels. This combination of inbound and outbound distribution created balanced growth that did not depend entirely on paid acquisition or viral mechanics critical for a marketplace where both supply and demand sides needed simultaneous scaling.

The third strategic element involved positioning Faire not simply as a marketplace or software tool but as a business partner aligned with independent retail success. The narrative they built emphasized supporting local businesses against Amazon and big-box retail competition, championing independent retail culture, and providing infrastructure that leveled the playing field between small stores and major chains. This positioning resonated emotionally with retailers who saw themselves fighting for survival against larger competitors, and it resonated practically because Faire's business model genuinely aligned with retailer success. They made money when retailers sold products, not from listing fees or subscriptions, creating a shared incentive structure that was not purely transactional.

INTEGRATED EXECUTION

The execution unfolded across three phases that demonstrated how product, distribution, and positioning create multiplicative rather than additive value. The first phase spanned 2017 through 2019. It focused on proving product-market fit and retention economics within core categories like home goods and gifts, where independent retailers had the strongest differentiation opportunity against online competitors.

During this period, they validated that an exceptional product experience, as measured by retention rates, could coexist with proactive distribution. They proved that inside sales did not cheapen the brand or suggest that the product was not self-evidently valuable, but instead reached customer segments that needed education before adopting.

Their positioning as champions of independent retail began to resonate as retailers recognized that Faire's success depended on theirs, creating trust that pure marketplace platforms struggled to establish.

The second phase, 2019 through 2021, tested whether their model could scale across categories and geographies while maintaining the integration of product, distribution, and positioning. They expanded from home goods into apparel, beauty, wellness, and other verticals where wholesale inefficiencies persisted. They launched in Europe and Canada, adapting their positioning to local independent retail cultures while maintaining a core narrative of supporting small businesses.

Critically, they maintained retention metrics even as they scaled. Net revenue retention remained above 130% even as they crossed the 100,000-retailer account mark. This proved that product excellence was not diluted by geographic or category expansion. Their distribution approach evolved to include retailer referrals and brand-driven acquisition as network effects began to take hold, but they maintained sales team investment rather than assuming growth would become entirely self-sustaining. GMV crossed $500 million annually, then $1 billion, demonstrating that exceptional retention, combined with deliberate distribution, could drive sustainable growth at scale.

The third phase began in 2021 when they raised $400 million in Series G at $12.4 billion valuation, making Faire one of the highest-valued private marketplaces globally. This valuation reflected investor recognition that they had solved the three-sided challenge: a product that created genuine retention (net revenue retention above 130%), a distribution that could reach and convert independent retailers efficiently (a combination of inbound and sales-driven), and a positioning that created brand moat and customer loyalty beyond functional utility.

💡 THE LESSON

Faire's trajectory validates this chapter's central argument that product does not win alone, and that exceptional product quality lays a foundation that must be amplified through deliberate distribution-building and strategic positioning. Analyzing through the integrated lens reveals how each element reinforced the others. Product features like net-30 terms and free returns were not just convenience but retention mechanisms that supported distribution by reducing sales friction. Positioning as a partner to independent retail made distribution more effective by making sales conversations less transactional, and distribution investment allowed them to reach retailers who would have missed exceptional products through passive discovery alone.

The case demonstrates that, in marketplace businesses, retention metrics validate product excellence but do not drive growth on their own. You need distribution to reach both sides of the marketplace and positioning to create trust and loyalty beyond functional utility. Most critically for founders, Faire illustrates that the three forces work multiplicatively: velocity in product improvement (shipping features weekly) created a better experience that supported distribution efficiency; momentum from retention (130%+ net revenue retention) made distribution spending sustainable; and distribution channels reached customers who accelerated momentum through repeat behavior.

The memorable synthesis: Faire built exceptional product with 130%+ net revenue retention, but scaled to $12+ billion valuation and $500 million+ GMV because they understood product excellence creates necessary foundation that must be amplified through deliberate distribution building (sales team plus inbound marketing) and strategic positioning (partner to independent retail, not just marketplace), proving that $V \cap M \cap D$ in practice means great product plus distribution plus positioning, not great product hoping distribution and positioning emerge organically.

The lesson is clear: building a great product is necessary, but not sufficient. Retention, engagement, and workflow integration create compounding advantages, but those advantages only matter if the product reaches the right users and resonates with them.

Key Takeaways

This chapter's argument converges into a few governing dynamics around retention:

- Retention is the foundation of sustainable growth. Value compounds when customers stay: their usage generates data that improves the product, repeated interaction builds habits that make switching harder, and deeper workflow integration makes replacement costly. Without retention, companies are forced to buy growth over and over just to stand still.
- The frequency and depth of engagement matter more than the breadth of features, because products used daily create stronger habits and generate more data than those used occasionally.
- Network effects are powerful but rare and difficult to engineer, requiring careful design of interactions that make the product genuinely more valuable as more people use it.

- Product expansion should follow natural usage patterns rather than force additional features onto customers who do not need them, as forced expansion often damages the core value proposition.

The next challenge is ensuring that the market understands and recognizes that how a company positions itself, tells its story, and establishes category leadership can amplify or diminish the compounding power of a product.

Chapter 5

Marketing in a World of Infinite Noise

Market positioning becomes self-reinforcing when category leadership attracts customers, talent, and partnerships that further strengthen leadership in a compounding cycle that competitors struggle to break.

— *Jim Collins, Good to Great*

The Collapse of Attention Economics

The fundamental challenge facing marketing today is not a lack of channels, tools, or tactics. Every possible marketing platform exists, every tool is available, and every playbook has been written and shared. The problem is more structural: attention has become genuinely scarce while the supply of content, messages, and advertising has become effectively infinite.

The central argument of this chapter is simple but uncomfortable: performance marketing has not stopped working, but it has stopped working alone. The companies that win in the next decade will not abandon paid acquisition, but they will subordinate it to systems that compound trust, narrative, and community over time.

If attention has truly become scarce, then the economic model built on buying and interrupting that attention deserves closer scrutiny. The consequences of this shift are most visible not in theory, but in the deteriorating economics of performance marketing itself.

The Limits of Performance Marketing

Traditional performance marketing, built on paid acquisition through platforms like Facebook, Google, and

TikTok, faces structurally rising costs and declining effectiveness. Customer acquisition costs have risen dramatically across nearly every vertical as more companies compete for the same limited attention. The platforms themselves take increasing percentages of the value created, leaving thinner margins for the companies doing the acquiring. Perhaps more importantly, users become adept at ignoring interruptive advertising. They scroll past ads instinctively, distrust claims reflexively, and increasingly rely on peer recommendations rather than brands. The result is not that performance marketing is dead, but that its economics are far less forgiving than they once were.

Rising acquisition costs and declining conversion rates are symptoms, not root causes. Beneath them lies a deeper shift: audiences are no longer deciding what to engage with based on exposure alone, but on whether the source feels credible, aligned, and worth believing.

Trust as the Scarce Resource

While attention has become scarce, trust has become even more valuable and more difficult to earn. Consumers and business buyers alike have been repeatedly burned by products that overpromised and underdelivered, by companies that prioritized growth over customer value, and by influencers and publications that recommended products primarily because of affiliate relationships. The result is widespread skepticism toward any marketing message that resembles traditional advertising, even when the advertised product is genuinely good.

This shift has profound implications for how startups should think about marketing strategy. Building trust requires approaches that are fundamentally different from buying attention. Trust is built through consistency over time, transparency about trade-offs and limitations, delivery on promises, education rather than persuasion, and demonstrated expertise rather than claims. Trust accumulates slowly but compounds powerfully once established. A company that has earned genuine trust can launch new products, enter new markets, and withstand setbacks in ways that companies dependent on paid acquisition cannot.

Since trust is the cumulative result of how a company shows up in every interaction, the real challenge is no longer choosing the right tools but orchestrating them into a coherent system.

From Tactics to Systems: The Integration Imperative

The defining challenge of modern marketing is not tactic selection but system integration. Most companies have access to the same tools: email, paid acquisition, content, PR, partnerships, community platforms, and product-led growth loops. The difference between companies that compound and those that stall lies in whether these elements reinforce one another or operate as disconnected initiatives optimized for local metrics.

Without a unifying strategy, each function succeeds locally while the system fails globally. The replacement for performance-only marketing is not brand, content, or community in isolation, but an integrated system designed to compound trust over time.

Once marketing is understood as a system rather than a collection of tactics, certain levers take on new importance, not as isolated strategies, but as interdependent components that shape how trust is formed, reinforced, and transferred over time.

Brand, Content, and Community as a Single System

Rather than separate disciplines, brand, content, and community function as interlocking layers of the same trust-building system. Brand defines what you stand for, content demonstrates that stance through useful knowledge, and community allows customers to carry it forward.

Brand is not logos, color schemes, or design systems, though those matter. Brand is the set of associations, perceptions, and emotional responses that people have when they encounter your company. It is what makes one product feel safer, more credible, or more valuable than another with similar features and pricing. Brand earns forgiveness when things go wrong and justifies premium pricing when they go right.

Content, when done well, becomes a compounding asset. Unlike paid advertising, which stops delivering once spending stops, content continues to generate value through discovery, sharing, and references. A strong content library does not persuade but educates, clarifies, and reduces uncertainty.

Community turns trust into distribution. A genuine community of users creates social proof, peer support, feedback loops, and advocacy that no paid channel can replicate. Community does not scale quickly, but it scales deeply.

These elements are not substitutes for performance marketing. They are force multipliers that make every paid dollar more effective.

Among these components, content plays a unique role: it is often the first place where a company's beliefs are tested against reality, and where trust is either earned through usefulness or lost through irrelevance.

Content as a Compounding Asset

Content marketing, when done well, functions as a compounding asset that creates value long after the initial creation. A well-written piece of content that ranks for relevant search terms or gets shared within a professional community continues to drive traffic, leads, and awareness for months or years. This is fundamentally different from paid advertising, which stops delivering results the moment you stop paying. The investment in content compounds over time as you build a library of material that covers your domain comprehensively.

Stripe built significant brand and distribution advantages through its content approach. Their documentation was so good that it became the standard that other companies tried to match. Their engineering blog published thoughtful pieces about how they solved complex problems, building credibility with their core developer audience. Their economic research and writing on the state of online business positioned them as thought leaders beyond being merely a payment processor. None of this was directly measurable in the same way that advertising spend and conversion rates are, yet it created substantial value by building trust, driving organic discovery, and differentiating Stripe from competitors.

The challenge with content marketing is that most companies do it poorly. They create generic content optimized for search engines rather than humans. They write about what they think they should write about rather than what their audience actually wants to know. They treat content as a checkbox activity rather than a strategic investment that requires real creativity and insight. Bad content is arguably worse than no content, as it wastes resources and can damage brand perception.

When content consistently delivers value, it does more than inform. It creates shared understanding. Over time, that shared understanding becomes the foundation upon which relationships form, enabling community to emerge naturally rather than being artificially engineered.

Community as Trust Infrastructure

Community building has become one of the most powerful but least understood marketing strategies for certain types of companies. A genuine community of users who care about your product, interact with one another, and identify with your brand creates network effects on awareness and acquisition.

Notion built its growth significantly through the community. Their ambassador program turned passionate users into evangelists who created templates, tutorials, and content that helped new users and drove awareness. Their online communities on platforms such as Reddit and Discord became places where users helped one another and shared use cases, creating a self-sustaining ecosystem that generated growth without direct company intervention.

Building genuine community is exceptionally difficult and cannot be manufactured through superficial tactics. It requires building a product that people genuinely care about enough to want to connect with others who use it. It requires giving the community real value, whether through access, recognition, or substantive benefits. It requires sustained engagement and authentic interaction rather than treating the community as a marketing channel to be exploited.

Yet, even the strongest communities deteriorate when they sense manipulation or misalignment. Sustained trust requires something deeper than engagement mechanics: it requires authenticity that holds up under repeated exposure.

Authenticity as Competitive Advantage

In a world where everyone is constantly marketing, and every message is suspect, authenticity has become a genuine competitive advantage. Companies that are willing to be transparent about their challenges, that admit what they do not do well, that share their thinking even when it makes them vulnerable, build trust that is difficult for competitors to match. This does not mean oversharing or treating customers as therapists. It means being honest in your positioning, being clear about whom you serve and whom you do not, and being willing to take positions that might alienate some people in order to resonate more deeply with others.

Basecamp built its entire brand on being opinionated and somewhat contrarian about project management and company building. They alienated customers who wanted enterprise features and extensive customization, but they built strong loyalty among customers who resonated with their philosophy. Their marketing consisted of sharing their opinions on how work should be done, which cost little but created a deep connection with the right audience.

Authenticity cannot be optimized for speed. It resists short-term measurement and demands consistency over time, forcing companies to confront an uncomfortable reality about what sustainable marketing actually requires.

The Long Game and Its Constraints

The uncomfortable truth about modern marketing is that most of what works takes time to compound. Brand builds slowly. Content libraries accumulate. Communities grow organically. Trust develops through consistency. None of these fit neatly into quarterly planning cycles or demand immediate measurable ROI. This creates tension between what actually works and what companies feel pressured to do: generate immediate, measurable results that justify continued investment.

The companies that win in marketing over the long term are those willing to invest in assets that compound even when the short-term returns are difficult to measure. They balance performance marketing, which delivers immediate results, with brand-building and content creation that pays off over the years. They recognize that marketing is not just about generating leads next quarter but about building durable advantages in trust, awareness, and positioning that make every subsequent dollar more effective.

Marketing in a world of infinite noise requires either massive spending that most startups cannot afford or building genuine differentiation through brand, community, content, and authentic connection with an audience. The tactics matter far less than the strategy, and the strategy must be about building compounding assets rather than executing campaigns. The companies that understand this and have the patience to build properly will compound their advantages, while competitors pursue temporary tactics that appear strong in monthly metrics but build nothing lasting.

These trade-offs become most visible in markets where trust is fragile and attention is expensive, making theory insufficient on its own. Cowrywise offers a concrete example of how long-term trust-building can function not as a supporting tactic, but as the core growth engine.

🔍 *Case Study - Cowrywise*

When Financial Education Becomes Marketing Strategy

In 2017, when Razaq Ahmed founded Cowrywise in Lagos, Nigeria, the African fintech and savings market was becoming increasingly crowded with noise: traditional banks like GTBank, Access Bank, and First Bank dominated financial services with extensive branch networks and massive marketing budgets, microfinance institutions served lower-income segments with savings products, digital lenders like Carbon (formerly Paylater) and FairMoney were gaining traction with instant loans marketed through aggressive social media campaigns, and investment platforms like Bamboo and Chaka were launching to serve young Africans wanting to invest in US stocks. The category featured hundreds of competitors, all promising similar benefits: better returns, easier access, lower fees, mobile-first experience, making differentiation through traditional advertising nearly impossible.

Yet, the existing solutions missed a fundamental insight about the Nigerian market that every young professional understood but few financial services companies addressed: the primary barrier to saving and investing was not lack of access to products but lack of financial literacy, trust in financial institutions after numerous Ponzi schemes, and behavioral challenges of consistent saving in a cash-based economy with social pressure to spend. Traditional banks offered savings accounts but required minimum balances that excluded many young people and provided interest rates below inflation. Investment platforms focused on stock trading but assumed users understood asset allocation, risk management, and investment fundamentals. Digital lenders marketed quick credit but contributed to debt cycles rather than wealth building.

Ahmed, who had worked in financial services and had witnessed how financially capable young Africans struggled to save and invest despite good intentions, recognized that the opportunity was not just about building a better savings app. Though Cowrywise's automated savings features became renowned for their behavioral psychology application, creating educational movement where financial literacy itself became the marketing strategy that cut through noise. This was not with advertising spend, but with genuine value that built trust, community, and narrative resonating with young Africans who wanted to build wealth but did not know how. In the world of infinite noise, where every fintech advertised disrupting finance with technology, Cowrywise needed a marketing approach that addressed the real barrier: knowledge and trust, not product features.

BUILDING TRUST THROUGH FINANCIAL EDUCATION

Cowrywise's approach demonstrated how marketing in noisy markets can create a competitive moat by leading with education that builds trust before requesting customer commitment. The first strategic pillar involved creating comprehensive financial literacy content that provided genuine value independent of product adoption. They launched "Ope's Money Diary" podcast that captured the everyday reflections, challenges, and triumphs of a young Nigerian navigating life, money, and meaning.

Episodes addressed real financial questions Nigerian millennials faced, such as how to save for rent when landlords demand an annual payment, how to invest small amounts consistently, how to build an emergency fund on irregular income, and how to resist family pressure to spend rather than save. The practical, culturally-relevant advice built trust with an audience that had been burned by Ponzi schemes and bank failures, establishing the Cowrywise team as credible financial educators before introducing them as product builders. This content-first approach created marketing that did not feel like marketing: listeners discovered the podcast through recommendations from friends who genuinely found it valuable, not through paid advertising.

The second pillar involved building community around shared financial goals rather than transactional product relationships. They created "Cowrywise Tribes," savings circles where groups of users committed to collective goals like saving for rent, building emergency funds, or starting investment portfolios. These Tribes featured leaderboards showing progress, group chats for motivation and accountability, and shared educational content relevant to each Tribe's goals. These community mechanics transformed saving from a solitary, shame-inducing activity into a collective movement with social support and celebration. When Tribe members hit savings goals, their success stories became testimonials more powerful than any advertisement: real people with similar incomes and circumstances demonstrating that consistent small savings accumulated into meaningful amounts.

The third pillar involved radical transparency about investment products, fees, and risks that built trust in a market where financial institutions historically exploited information asymmetry. They published detailed breakdowns of exactly where customer money was invested, including specific government securities and treasury bills with current yields. They explained all fees clearly before users committed funds. They created educational content explaining investment risks, including the potential for losses, market volatility, and liquidity constraints, rather than promising guaranteed returns as Ponzi schemes had.

This transparency created differentiation in the market where competitors marketed aggressively but hid important details in fine print: Cowrywise users understood exactly what they were buying, why certain investments offered higher returns (because they carried more risk), and what fees they paid for the service. When users asked questions on social media or in community forums, the Cowrywise team provided detailed educational responses rather than marketing copy, reinforcing its positioning as a financial education platform that prioritized user understanding over user acquisition. The transparency meant word-of-mouth recommendations included informed descriptions of product strengths and limitations rather than unrealistic expectations that created disappointment.

NARRATIVE AS INCLUSIVE WEALTH-BUILDING MOVEMENT

The execution unfolded across three phases that demonstrated how narrative and positioning cut through noise when established players dominate traditional channels. The first phase, 2017 through 2019, established the "making wealth-building accessible to every Nigerian" narrative that differentiated Cowrywise from both traditional banks and other fintechs. During this period, they made deliberate choices that reinforced inclusive positioning: allowing users to start saving with as little as ₦100 (less than $0.25), removing minimum balance requirements that excluded low-income users, building automated savings features that helped users save before spending rather than trying to save what remained, and creating investment portfolios that pooled small amounts to access institutional-grade securities typically available only to wealthy individuals.

The competitive landscape included traditional banks with savings accounts requiring minimum balances of ₦10,000-50,000 and offering negligible interest, investment firms serving high-net-worth individuals with minimums of ₦1 million+, and digital lenders marketing quick loans that often trapped users in debt cycles. Microfinance institutions served low-income segments, but often with exploitative interest rates and poor customer experience. Other savings apps existed, but they were marketed primarily on interest rates and features rather than on behavioral support and education. Cowrywise's narrative advantage became clear as young Nigerians making ₦50,000-200,000 monthly ($120-480) described it as the first financial service that actually seemed designed for people like them, not wealthy investors. This is because they tolerated small accounts, while genuinely building for the mass market with appropriate features, content, and community support.

The narrative created by inclusive positioning meant that on platforms where Cowrywise's target customers congregated, like Nigerian Twitter (now X), Facebook groups for young professionals, WhatsApp communities, and university networks, the product became a default recommendation even when others mentioned alternatives. Users described converting friends with missionary zeal because they genuinely felt they were helping people access wealth-building opportunities previously available only to the elite. The positioning as a financial inclusion movement rather than a savings product created an emotional connection beyond functional benefits, and users wanted Cowrywise to succeed as validation of their belief that ordinary Nigerians deserved access to quality financial services.

The second phase, 2019 through 2021, tested whether an educational-first narrative could scale beyond the initial early adopter community into the mainstream market while maintaining authentic positioning. They expanded the product suite beyond basic savings to dollar savings (addressing naira devaluation concerns), mutual fund investments with diversified portfolios, and, eventually, real estate investments through fractional property ownership. Each new product launched with comprehensive educational content explaining how it worked, who it suited, what risks existed, and how it fit into the overall financial plan. They raised seed funding from Quona Capital and other impact investors that enabled team expansion and product development while maintaining a marketing approach focused on education and community rather than paid advertising.

The challenge was maintaining narrative authenticity as the company scaled and competition intensified: would Cowrywise remain an educational movement that makes wealth-building accessible, or become just another fintech competing on interest rates and features? They navigated this by continuing to lead with education even as competitors launched with aggressive marketing campaigns. When inflation spiked and the Naira devalued sharply in 2020-2021, they published educational content explaining macroeconomic forces affecting savings and investments, rather than just promoting their dollar-savings product. When users lost money in mutual fund investments during market downturns, they created content explaining market volatility and long-term investment principles rather than hiding losses or making unrealistic promises.

The narrative evolution demonstrated how positioning can deepen over time when the core thesis proves correct: they extended "accessible wealth-building" from basic savings to comprehensive financial planning that included emergency funds, short-term savings goals, long-term investments across asset classes, and eventually insurance products, with a consistent philosophy that financial education enabled better decisions across all these areas. They launched Cowrywise for Business, offering corporate savings and investment products with the same transparent pricing and educational approach. They shared growth milestones: 100,000 users in 2019, 300,000+ by 2021, with a tone that celebrated collective financial progress rather than corporate achievement.

The third phase began around 2021 when Cowrywise's sustained growth through educational content and community building validated that knowledge-based marketing could create a competitive moat even in a market dominated by banks with massive advertising budgets and aggressive fintechs with venture capital to burn on user acquisition. They served 500,000+ users by 2023, managed billions of naira in customer assets, and maintained industry-leading retention rates despite facing competition from traditional banks, dozens of well-funded savings and investment apps, and international platforms entering the Nigerian market. They expanded into more sophisticated investment products, including diversified portfolios, sector-focused funds, and Halal investment options, each new product supported by comprehensive educational content.

Most critically, they demonstrated that narrative advantage compounds when product experience validates positioning: early adopters who learned financial fundamentals became lifetime advocates sharing knowledge with friends and family. Users who started with ₦1,000 monthly automated savings and watched it grow to ₦100,000+ over two years stayed with Cowrywise as they progressed to investments and real estate, because the platform had educated them throughout their financial journey. Young professionals who joined for savings features discovered that educational content helped them negotiate better salaries, make smarter spending decisions, and plan for major life goals, values that extended far beyond the product itself. The narrative of "making wealth-building accessible" that initially attracted financially curious millennials became a self-fulfilling prophecy as the user base's advocacy drove mainstream adoption, generating more word-of-mouth in a virtuous cycle that advertising could not replicate.

THE LESSON

Cowrywise validates that marketing in the world of infinite noise requires building trust through genuine value and education rather than projecting messages through paid campaigns. The case demonstrates that in emerging markets where trust is low and financial literacy is limited, the most effective marketing comes from leading with education that builds knowledge before requesting commitment. Most critically for founders, Cowrywise illustrates that cutting through noise requires addressing the real barriers to adoption, not product features or pricing, but understanding, trust, and behavior change, through content and community that provide genuine value independent of product usage.

Viewed through the lens of attention economics, Cowrywise's growth is less an exception than a signal, illustrating what becomes possible when education, transparency, and patience replace interruption as the primary marketing strategy.

Key Takeaways

Ultimately, advantage becomes self-reinforcing through position, not just execution.

- Category creation and leadership create compounding advantages by making your company the default and attracting ecosystem participants, especially in developer tools, marketplaces, and platforms.
- Positioning must be narrow enough to achieve genuine leadership in something specific before attempting to expand into adjacent categories.

- The narrative you tell about your product shapes not just customer perception but also internal execution as teams build what the positioning promises.
- Repositioning is possible but expensive, as it requires overcoming established mental models while competitors continue to build advantages in their positions.

All of these efforts raise a simpler, more consequential question: not whether a company can create value, but how reliably it can deliver that value to the market. The answer lies less in individual tactics than in the structures that determine who gets reached, how often, and at what cost. That shift, from execution to access, is where the next chapter begins.

Chapter 6

Distribution Is the Business

Distribution advantages compound because investments in channels, content, relationships, and brand make future customer acquisition progressively easier and more efficient over time.

— *Flynn Glover, Matcha*

The Misunderstood Moat

If you ask most founders what their competitive advantage is, they will talk about product features, technology, team quality, or market timing. Very few will identify distribution as their primary moat, yet distribution is often the most durable and defensible advantage a company can build. This reflects a fundamental misunderstanding about what actually determines business outcomes in competitive markets.

Distribution, properly understood, is not a marketing channel or a sales strategy. Distribution is the entire system through which a product reaches customers, delivers value, retains those customers, and expands within accounts or networks. Distribution is the strategic architecture that governs customer acquisition, activation, retention, and expansion. It is why companies with inferior products often beat those with superior products. This is why startups with brilliant technology sometimes fail, while competitors with mediocre technology scale successfully.

The most successful technology companies of the last two decades all built distribution advantages that competitors could not easily replicate. Amazon built a logistics infrastructure and a Prime membership that created a moat far stronger than any product selection or pricing advantage. Apple built retail stores that controlled the customer experience and created brand differentiation that went well beyond hardware specifications. Salesforce built a direct sales organization and an ecosystem of implementation partners that created switching costs and expansion dynamics beyond those provided by the software itself. In each case, the distribution system became more defensible than the product.

Once distribution is understood as an advantage rather than execution, the next question is not whether it matters, but what kind of distribution is worth building.

Owned Versus Rented Channels

One of the most critical strategic questions facing any startup is the extent to which its distribution will be through owned versus rented channels. Rented channels are platforms and systems controlled by others, where you pay for access and accept rules that may change at any time. Facebook ads, Google search, app store placement, and Amazon marketplace selling are all rented channels. They can be highly effective in the short term, but they are inherently unstable over the long term because the platform owner extracts increasing value over time and can change rules that destroy your business model overnight.

Owned channels are systems where you control the customer relationship directly. Email lists, direct website traffic, owned retail locations, and API integrations where you provide core infrastructure are owned channels. They are more difficult to build because they require creating value that leads customers to come to you directly, rather than discover you through a platform. But once built, they create durable advantages that platforms cannot easily disrupt.

The most sophisticated companies build hybrid distribution systems that use rented channels opportunistically while investing aggressively in owned channels that provide long-term stability. They might use paid advertising to acquire initial customers, then focus intensively on retention and word-of-mouth to drive organic growth that does not depend on continued platform spending. They might list products on Amazon to gain initial traction while simultaneously building direct-to-consumer channels that improve unit economics and customer relationships.

The trade-offs of rented distribution become clearest in platforms, where leverage is highest, and dependence is easiest to underestimate.

Platform Leverage and Risk

Platforms provide substantial leverage for companies that use them effectively, enabling small startups to access distribution that would otherwise require substantial capital and decades to build. A small e-commerce company can reach millions of potential customers through Amazon. A new app can acquire users through social platform advertising. A B2B startup can generate leads through Google search. This platform leverage has enabled the creation of thousands of companies that could not have existed in previous eras.

However, this leverage comes with existential risk that many founders underestimate until it is too late. Platforms change their algorithms, their fee structures, and their policies in ways that can overnight destroy business models built on top of them. Facebook has repeatedly changed its algorithm in ways that decimated businesses built on organic reach. Apple changed IDFA tracking rules in ways that dramatically increased mobile app acquisition costs. Amazon increases fees and launches competing products that undermine sellers in its marketplace.

Companies that depend primarily on rented platforms for distribution are building on unstable ground. They may grow quickly by exploiting platform mechanics, but that growth is fragile and can evaporate when platform incentives change. The strategic imperative is to use platform distribution to build owned distribution, moving customers into direct relationships where possible, building brand recognition that creates customer preference beyond platform discovery, and diversifying across multiple channels so that no single platform has undue power over the business.

Not all external distribution carries the same risk, however, particularly when access is earned through integration rather than purchased through platforms.

Partnerships as a Distribution Strategy

Strategic partnerships are among the most powerful but also among the most difficult to execute distribution strategies. A partnership with a company that already has access to your target customers can provide distribution that would take years to build independently. Stripe grew in part through partnerships with platforms such as Shopify, where it became the default payment processor, providing access to hundreds of thousands of merchants. Twilio grew through partnerships and integrations with applications that needed a communication infrastructure. These partnerships created distribution leverage that pure marketing approaches could not match.

The challenge with partnership distribution is that meaningful partnerships are extraordinarily difficult to negotiate and execute. The partner needs to have strong incentives to promote your product over alternatives. The integration needs to be tight enough that the partnership creates real value rather than being merely nominal. The economics must work for both parties sustainably. Many founders spend substantial time pursuing partnerships that never materialize or fail to generate meaningful volume even after signing.

The most effective partnership strategies focus on creating dynamics in which both parties mutually benefit from the relationship's success. This often means being willing to share economics generously enough that the partner is genuinely motivated to sustain the relationship. It means investing in integration quality that makes the partnership seamless for end customers. It means ongoing relationship management that ensures the partnership continues to generate value for both sides as circumstances change.

Ecosystems as Compounding Distribution

As partnerships expand beyond one-to-one relationships and begin to repeat at scale, distribution starts to compound in new ways. Over time, these repeated integrations can give rise to ecosystems in which third parties extend the product and drive adoption without requiring a proportional investment from the company. Salesforce built the AppExchange, where thousands of developers extended the platform, creating integrations and applications that made Salesforce more valuable and harder to leave. Shopify has built an ecosystem of themes, apps, and service providers that help merchants succeed, creating a network effect in which more merchants attract more ecosystem partners, which in turn attract more merchants.

Building an ecosystem requires reaching a sufficient scale that third parties perceive an opportunity to build on your platform. It requires providing APIs, documentation, economic incentives, and support that make ecosystem participation attractive. It requires managing the ecosystem to maintain quality and prevent bad actors from damaging the customer experience. When implemented well, ecosystem development creates compounding returns, with your distribution improving automatically as more participants invest in building on your platform.

The challenge is that building ecosystems is primarily available to companies that have already achieved meaningful scale. Early-stage startups rarely have the leverage to build true ecosystems, though they can position themselves to eventually create ecosystem dynamics once they reach sufficient scale. The strategic question for early companies is whether their product architecture and business model create the potential for ecosystem formation once they reach scale.

Direct Sales as a Distribution System

For many B2B companies, particularly those selling to enterprises, direct sales represent the primary distribution channel. Building a sales organization that can consistently acquire customers at reasonable economics is one of the most difficult challenges in scaling a business. Sales is not just about hiring people who can close deals. It concerns developing a repeatable system for identifying prospects, creating opportunities, managing pipelines, and closing business at predictable rates and deal sizes.

Companies that scale successfully through direct sales do so by methodically defining their sales process and then hiring people who can execute it consistently. They identify their ideal customer profile precisely enough that sellers focus on high-probability prospects rather than waste time on poor fits. They develop messaging and positioning that resonates with their market. They develop supporting materials and case studies that enhance the sales process. They design compensation structures that align sellers' incentives with organizational goals.

The mistake many founders make with sales is assuming that hiring experienced sellers will solve their distribution problems. If the founder cannot sell the product themselves, if the positioning and pricing have not been validated, and if the sales process has not been mapped out, hiring salespeople will not address the underlying problems. The best practice is for founders to conduct initial sales themselves until they understand the process deeply enough to teach it to others, then hire salespeople to scale what already works rather than to determine what works.

Direct sales embeds distribution through people and process. In contrast, some products embed distribution directly into usage itself, allowing adoption to spread through how the product is used rather than how it is sold.

Product-Led Growth as Distribution

Product-led growth treats the product itself as the primary distribution mechanism. Instead of relying on sales teams or external channels to drive adoption, growth emerges from how the product is discovered, adopted, and shared through normal use. Companies like Slack, Zoom, Dropbox, and Calendly grew primarily through users adopting the product and then inviting colleagues or sharing outputs that drove viral acquisition. This approach can yield better unit economics than sales-driven models because customer acquisition occurs through product usage rather than through costly marketing or sales processes.

Product-led growth requires designing distribution directly into the product architecture from the beginning. The product must have natural sharing or collaboration dynamics that create viral loops. The value must be obvious enough that users want to invite others without being asked. The free tier must provide sufficient value to encourage organic adoption while creating clear upgrade paths to paid tiers. The onboarding must be frictionless enough that people who discover the product through sharing can adopt it immediately without requiring sales assistance.

The challenge with product-led growth is that it only works for certain types of products in which collaboration or sharing is natural. Enterprise software that requires significant implementation or customization cannot typically rely on pure product-led growth. Complex products with long learning curves struggle to create the immediate value that drives viral sharing. The strategy is powerful when it fits the product, but cannot be imposed on products whose dynamics do not naturally support it.

Distribution as an Integrated System

The critical insight is that distribution is not a single channel or tactic but an integrated system in which different elements reinforce one another. The best companies use multiple distribution channels simultaneously, understanding how they interact and support each other. They might acquire initial customers through content marketing, retain them through product excellence, expand within accounts through product-led growth dynamics, and then use those successful customers as references for direct sales into larger enterprises.

Building this kind of integrated distribution system requires seeing distribution as a core strategic priority rather than a tactical execution problem. It requires investment across multiple channels simultaneously, even when short-term returns are uncertain. It requires patience to let distribution advantages compound over time rather than expecting immediate returns.

The companies that will dominate their markets are not necessarily those with the best products but those with the most sophisticated distribution systems. Distribution advantages compound over time as channels mature, ecosystems develop, brands strengthen, and owned audiences grow. These advantages become moats that competitors cannot easily cross, regardless of product quality.

Distribution is not what you do after you build a product. Distribution is the business. It is part of the product strategy from day one. Companies that understand this and integrate distribution into their core strategy will compound their advantages and build defensible positions that last, whereas competitors that focus exclusively on product features will not.

 ## Case Study - Interswitch

When Owned Distribution Becomes an Unassailable Moat

In 2002, when Mitchell Elegbe founded Interswitch in Lagos, Nigeria, the country's payment infrastructure was effectively non-existent in digital form: banks operated isolated systems that could not communicate with each other, ATM networks were fragmented by institution, point-of-sale terminals were rare outside major cities, and the vast majority of commerce happened in cash because electronic payments were unreliable and limited to single-bank ecosystems. International payment networks like Visa and Mastercard served only the wealthy elite, leaving Nigeria's emerging middle class and small businesses without access to modern payment infrastructure.

The opportunity was obvious to multiple players: connect Nigeria's banking system, enable interbank transactions, build ATM networks that worked across institutions, and create payment rails for the digital economy everyone knew was coming. Yet, Elegbe's critical insight was not about building better payment technology. While the technical challenges were significant, they were ultimately solvable. His real insight was that in infrastructure businesses, whoever controls distribution controls the market, and that lasting advantage comes from building owned distribution channels that competitors cannot afford to replicate and customers cannot leave.

BUILDING OWNED DISTRIBUTION AS MOAT

Interswitch's strategy demonstrated how owned distribution transforms from a growth tactic into an existential business moat. The first strategic pillar involved building physical infrastructure that competitors could not easily duplicate: they deployed thousands of ATMs across Nigeria that ran on Interswitch's network, created point-of-sale terminal networks that merchants installed in stores, established

Quickteller agent locations in neighborhoods where formal banking did not reach, and built backend switching infrastructure that connected Nigeria's banks into a unified payment system.

Building this physical distribution network required a significant capital investment and substantial operational effort. Interswitch had to manage hardware deployment, agent relationships, merchant onboarding, regulatory compliance, and technical reliability across a country with challenging infrastructure. In return, the network created powerful switching costs and network effects that made Interswitch increasingly valuable and difficult to displace. Every additional ATM made their network more useful to cardholders, every additional merchant made their point-of-sale system more attractive to banks, and every additional agent location made Quickteller more accessible to consumers, creating a compounding distribution advantage that competitors starting from zero could not match.

The second strategic element focused on creating an owned payment card brand rather than relying entirely on international networks. They launched Verve, a Nigerian payment card that worked on Interswitch's infrastructure, giving them control over the full payment value chain from card issuance through transaction processing to merchant acceptance. This was not just nationalist branding but a distribution strategy that reduced dependence on Visa and Mastercard, captured more transaction value, and created additional switching costs as banks integrated Verve issuance into their systems and merchants installed Verve-acceptance terminals. By 2023, Verve had become the dominant payment card in Nigeria with over 40 million cards issued, demonstrating that owned distribution could compete with global brands when backed by superior local infrastructure.

The third pillar involved building digital distribution channels that complemented physical infrastructure: Quickteller platform for online bill payments, mobile apps for consumer transactions, API infrastructure for developer integration, and B2B partnerships with banks and fintechs that wanted to leverage Interswitch's payment rails. These digital channels created additional distribution touchpoints while reinforcing the core infrastructure moat. Developers built applications on Interswitch's APIs, driving transaction volume through their network. Merchants who used Quickteller for bill collection became dependent on their infrastructure. Banks that had deeply integrated with Interswitch's systems found switching to competitors to be prohibitively disruptive.

DISTRIBUTION COMPOUNDS OVER TIME

The execution unfolded across three phases, demonstrating how owned distribution creates compounding competitive advantage. The first phase, 2002-2010, focused on building foundational infrastructure and achieving critical mass in core distribution channels. They deployed ATM networks across major Nigerian cities, onboarded banks onto the switching platform, established Quickteller agent networks in thousands of locations, and processed initial transaction volumes that validated the business model. During this period, capital intensity and operational complexity served as barriers to entry: competitors attempting to replicate Interswitch's distribution footprint faced multi-year timelines and substantial capital requirements merely to reach parity. Their B2B retention rates exceeded 90% as banks that integrated with Interswitch found switching costs around reintegrating systems, retraining staff, explaining changes to customers, prohibitively expensive relative to any incremental benefits competitors might offer.

The second phase, 2010-2018, tested whether owned distribution could sustain a competitive advantage as mobile money, fintech startups, and international payment companies entered the Nigerian market with different distribution strategies. Companies like Paga built mobile money networks, startups like Paystack offered developer-friendly payment APIs, and Mastercard and Visa expanded their presence in Nigeria. Yet Interswitch's distribution moat held because physical infrastructure and deep bank integrations created barriers digital-first competitors could not overcome quickly: their ATM network and POS terminals gave them presence in every major commercial location, their Quickteller agents reached neighborhoods where smartphone penetration remained low, and their position as backend switching infrastructure for Nigerian banking system made them embedded in critical financial flows that new entrants could not easily disintermediate. Transaction volumes grew to tens of billions of dollars annually as the firm expanded regionally into other African markets.

The third phase began around 2018 when Interswitch's valuation reached $1 billion in private funding rounds, making it one of Africa's first technology unicorns, with transaction volumes exceeding $120 billion annually processed through its infrastructure. This valuation reflected investor recognition that owned distribution had created nearly unassailable competitive position: their physical and digital distribution network was prohibitively expensive to replicate, their deep integrations with banks created switching costs measured in years of re-implementation work, their Verve card network had achieved scale where network effects reinforced market position, and their operational track record of 20+ years demonstrated staying power startups could not claim.

💡 THE LESSON

Interswitch's growth validates that distribution is the business, particularly in infrastructure markets where owned distribution channels create compounding advantages that product quality alone cannot generate. Also, Interswitch's ATM network was not just a distribution channel for payment products; it was the product that created value and defensibility.

For founders, the lesson is straightforward. Companies that rely on rented distribution like app stores, paid advertising, or partner referrals, must keep paying to maintain customer access. Companies that build owned distribution, including physical infrastructure, agent networks, and proprietary platforms, create assets that appreciate rather than depreciate over time.

Key Takeaways

The key takeaways in this chapter can therefore be summarized as follows:

- Distribution is often the most durable competitive advantage because it is hardest to replicate, takes the longest to build, and continues delivering value long after initial investments.
- Earned distribution compounds over time through content, SEO, brand, and word-of-mouth, as accumulated authority and trust reduce reliance on paid acquisition and make it harder for competitors to replicate quickly.
- Embedded distribution, through sales relationships, partnerships, platforms, and ecosystems, creates switching costs and dependencies that make displacement difficult even when competitors build superior products.

As advantages compound and structures solidify, a different tension comes into focus; one that has less to do with what is built and more to do with how it is built over time. Not every decision benefits from speed, and not every delay is prudent. The challenge shifts from choosing the right levers to developing judgment about when to move deliberately and when to act decisively. That tension defines the next phase.

Chapter 7

Systems Beat Campaigns

Strategic patience about building compounding advantages must coexist with tactical urgency in execution, requiring judgment about which decisions deserve deliberation and which demand immediate action.

— Jim Collins, Built to Last

The Campaign Mindset Trap

Most startups approach growth with a campaign mindset, organizing their efforts around discrete initiatives with defined beginning and end points. They plan a launch campaign, run a paid advertising campaign, execute a content campaign, and then move on to the next campaign without considering how these discrete efforts connect or compound over time.

This approach creates several structural problems.

- First, it prioritizes immediate, measurable results over building assets that compound over time.
- Second, it creates discontinuity, whereby momentum from one effort does not transfer to the next.
- Third, it prevents the sustained focus required for complex initiatives to succeed.
- Fourth, and most importantly, it fails to create the feedback loops and interconnections that transform isolated tactics into compounding systems.

The alternative is systems thinking. Systems are composed of interconnected components whose outputs reinforce one another. Campaigns fade because they must be recreated each time to achieve similar results. Systems compound because learning, data, and behavior accumulate.

The Architecture of Growth Systems

An effective growth system integrates product, channels, messaging, data, and feedback loops into a cohesive whole. The product is designed with built-in growth mechanisms that create natural incentives for users to share, invite others, or expand their use. The channels through which users discover the product are optimized not only for volume but also for quality, attracting users likely to retain and derive value from the product. The messaging resonates with the target audience in ways that create emotional connection and clear differentiation rather than merely listing features. The data infrastructure captures what matters and makes it visible to everyone who needs it, enabling fast learning and continuous optimization. The feedback loops ensure that learning flows back into product development, messaging refinement, and channel optimization, creating continuous improvement rather than static tactics.

Consider how HubSpot built a growth system rather than relying on campaigns. Their inbound marketing methodology was not just a marketing message but a complete system. They created educational content that attracted their target audience of marketers and business owners seeking better ways to generate leads. That content built authority and trust while capturing contact information. The content was optimized for search and sharing, creating compounding returns as their library grew. They built free tools that provided immediate value while demonstrating the capabilities of their paid products. The free tools generated qualified leads who already understood the product category and the problems it solved. Their product was designed to grow with customer success, expanding from simple landing pages to full marketing suites as customers' needs and sophistication grew. Each component reinforced the others, creating a system that generated growth more effectively than any single campaign could have achieved.

Product as System Component

In a proper growth system, the product is not separate from distribution but rather the central component that enables all other elements to work. The product needs to create value quickly enough that acquisition efforts are not wasted on users who churn before experiencing the core benefit. The product needs to have natural expansion and sharing dynamics built into its core functionality rather than bolted on as afterthoughts. The product must generate data and signals that inform the operation of other parts of the system.

Notion exemplifies how a product can be designed as the central component of a growth system. The product allows users to create public pages that can be shared, turning every user into a potential distribution channel. Templates created by power users serve as onboarding tools that help new users understand possibilities, while simultaneously driving acquisition as users discover Notion through templates. The product improves with use as users build up their workspaces, creating switching costs that enhance retention. The product's flexibility enables different users to solve distinct problems, generating word-of-mouth across multiple use cases simultaneously. None of these are isolated. They are interconnected elements of a product designed to enable system-level growth.

Channel Integration and Compounding

Growth systems integrate multiple channels in ways that reinforce one another rather than compete for budget. Content marketing builds organic visibility, thereby improving the efficiency of paid channels by creating brand recognition before the first paid impression. Direct sales benefit from product-led growth by engaging with accounts in which product adoption has already begun organically. Community efforts generate content and word-of-mouth that reduce acquisition costs across all channels.

Partnerships provide distribution that enhances the effectiveness of other channels by expanding reach and credibility.

The mistake most companies make is treating channels as independent and optimizing each one in isolation. They have a content person optimizing for traffic, a performance marketer optimizing for conversion rates, a sales team optimizing for deal closure, and a community manager optimizing for engagement. Each function achieves its local metrics, yet the overall system remains suboptimal because interactions between channels are ignored.

Building effective channel integration requires shared objectives that span functions, prompting teams to consider how their work enables other channels to be more effective. It requires attribution models that recognize when multiple channels contribute to an outcome rather than crediting only the last touch. It requires regular communication between teams working across different channels to ensure they understand how their efforts interact. Most importantly, it requires leadership that thinks holistically rather than managing each function independently.

As channels become more interconnected, intuition alone is no longer sufficient. At that point, the limiting factor is no longer effort or coordination, but the ability to see what is actually happening across the system.

Data as System Infrastructure

In a growth system, data is not merely a measurement but an essential infrastructure that enables continuous self-optimization. The data layer captures user behavior, channel performance, retention patterns, and product usage in ways that create feedback loops informing every part of the system. Product teams see which acquisition sources produce users with the highest retention and can prioritize features that serve those segments. Marketing teams see which messages and channels drive the most valuable customers and can allocate budget accordingly. Sales teams can see which product usage patterns predict expansion and prioritize outreach to accounts that exhibit those patterns.

The challenge is to build a data infrastructure that captures what matters without overwhelming teams with irrelevant metrics. This requires clarity about the key questions the business needs to answer, the instruments used to answer those questions, and discipline to ignore data that is merely interesting rather than actionable. It requires making data accessible to everyone who needs it rather than locking it away in analytics teams that produce reports nobody uses. It requires building dashboards and alerts that surface important changes without requiring constant manual monitoring.

The companies that build superior data infrastructure gain compounding advantages in learning speed. They identify what is working and what is not faster than their competitors. They adapt to market changes more quickly. They optimize their systems continuously rather than waiting for quarterly reviews to make adjustments. Data becomes a competitive advantage not because they have more of it, but because they translate it into decisions and actions more quickly.

Feedback Loops as System Core

The defining characteristic of systems versus campaigns is the presence of tight feedback loops that create continuous learning and improvement. In a campaign mindset, you plan an initiative, execute it, measure the results at the end, learn from the results, and then start planning the next separate campaign. In a systems mindset, feedback flows continuously, with each component providing information that improves other components in real-time.

Spotify's discovery algorithms create feedback loops between user listening behavior and content recommendations. The more users listen, the better the recommendations become. Better recommendations drive more listening. More listening generates more data. More data improves the algorithms. Each improvement increases the product's value, which drives retention, which generates more data, creating a virtuous cycle. This is not a campaign. It is a system that gets better automatically as it operates.

Building effective feedback loops requires instrumenting to capture the right signals, creating mechanisms that translate signals into actions, and giving teams the authority to make changes based on what they learn without requiring extensive approval processes. It requires rapid deployment cycles to enable timely action on insights before they become stale. It requires a culture that values learning over being right, where teams are encouraged to test hypotheses and adjust based on evidence rather than defending initial plans.

System Maintenance and Evolution

Growth systems require active maintenance and evolution as the business scales and market conditions change. What works at 10,000 users may not work at 1,000,000. Efficient channels become saturated. Product dynamics that initially drove growth may become less effective as you move into different customer segments. The system needs to evolve while maintaining the fundamental architecture that underpins its effectiveness.

This evolution is fundamentally different from the campaign mindset of constantly trying new tactics. In systems thinking, components are refined while maintaining the core architecture and feedback loops. You might add new channels to the system, but you integrate them properly rather than running them as independent experiments. You might adjust your messaging based on what you learn, but maintain consistency in your positioning. You might expand the product, but you preserve the growth mechanisms that made the original version successful.

The companies that scale successfully are those that transition from campaign thinking to systems thinking early enough to build infrastructure rather than merely execute tactics. They invest in the unglamorous work of instrumentation, integration, and feedback loops. They resist the temptation to chase every new channel or tactic and instead focus on building a system that generates consistent results.

Systems outperform campaigns because they compound, whereas campaigns fade. Systems create leverage while campaigns create work. Systems get stronger as they mature, while campaigns require constant reinvention. The shift from campaign thinking to systems thinking is one of the most important transitions a startup must make, and those that make it early build advantages that become increasingly difficult for competitors to overcome. The companies that dominate their markets are not those running the most clever campaigns but those building the most sophisticated systems.

The consequences of failing to shift from campaigns to systems are easiest to see not in theory, but in practice, especially when resources, talent, and attention are abundant. In those conditions, the absence of a system is often masked until growth collapses.

🔍 *Case Study - Quibi*

When $1.75 Billion Cannot Compensate for Missing Systems

In April 2020, Jeffrey Katzenberg and Meg Whitman launched Quibi, short for "quick bites". It was a mobile-first streaming service delivering premium short-form content designed for viewing in under ten minutes. They entered the market with advantages that most startups can only fantasize about: $1.75 billion in funding raised before launching a single product, a celebrity founder in Katzenberg who had run Disney Studios and co-founded DreamWorks Animation, and executive leadership in Whitman who had been CEO of eBay and HP. They secured content deals with Hollywood's top talent, including Steven Spielberg, Jennifer Lopez, and Liam Hemsworth, distribution partnerships with all major mobile platforms, and a marketing budget exceeding $470 million in the first year alone.

The product thesis seemed defensible: mobile viewing was growing rapidly, attention spans were fragmenting, commute time and idle moments created demand for content consumed in short bursts, and Gen Z audiences weren't being served by long-form streaming designed for television viewing. Quibi promised "movie-quality" storytelling in episodes under ten minutes, using proprietary "Turnstyle" technology that allowed seamless viewing in portrait or landscape orientation.

Yet, despite unprecedented resources, celebrity backing, premium content, and a massive marketing spend, Quibi shut down after just 6 months, having attracted only 500,000 paying subscribers from 4.5 million free-trial activations, with a retention rate under 12%, making the business model unsustainable at any scale. The failure demonstrated this chapter's central argument: campaigns without systems do not create sustainable growth, and having all three forces: velocity, momentum, and distribution, present but not integrated as a coherent system, produces expensive motion rather than compounding value.

CAMPAIGNS WITHOUT SYSTEMS

Quibi's approach exemplified how massive resource deployment without systematic integration can lead to failure despite apparent strengths. The first critical flaw involved treating product, marketing, and distribution as separate campaigns rather than an integrated system with feedback loops. They had a product in the form of a content library; 90+ shows at launch with new episodes releasing daily, premium Hollywood production values, and exclusive celebrity talent.

They had a massive marketing campaign, including Super Bowl commercials, billboards in major cities, social media advertising, influencer partnerships, and press coverage, treating the launch as a cultural moment. They had distribution through app stores with featured placement on iOS and Android, carrier partnerships with T-Mobile and Verizon bundling free trials, and a pre-launch waitlist that generated millions of sign-ups. Yet, these elements operated independently: marketing created awareness but did not inform product development based on what resonated with audiences, product released content on predetermined schedules without adapting to usage patterns, and distribution delivered app downloads but had no mechanism to improve conversion or retention based on user behavior.

The second critical failure involved mistaking campaign spending for system building, assuming that sufficient marketing investment would overcome structural product and retention challenges. The $470 million first-year marketing budget represented more than most startups raise in total funding, yet it bought temporary attention without creating compounding growth mechanisms.

Each dollar spent on Super Bowl ads or billboard placements generated one-time awareness that disappeared after the campaign ended, with no residual value or feedback loop that made subsequent marketing more efficient. They were not building a marketing system where early users became evangelists, where content generated word-of-mouth, and where product experience itself drove distribution. They were running an awareness campaign on a massive scale, which generated app downloads but did not create reasons for users to return after the initial trial or to recommend it to friends.

The third systemic flaw was the lack of feedback loops that connected user behavior to product evolution, making it impossible to iterate toward product-market fit despite real-time data on what was failing. They could see that retention was collapsing. For example, 91-day retention was under 10%, meaning 90%+ of users who tried Quibi abandoned it within 3 months. However, the content production model, which involved long lead times, Hollywood talent contracts, and episodic release schedules, made rapid iteration structurally impossible.

When users demonstrated they were not coming back for episodic short-form content, Quibi could not pivot to different content formats, viewing experiences, or value propositions. This was because the entire system, including the funding model, content partnerships, technology stack, and marketing messaging, was built around the original thesis. They had velocity in the form of content production and marketing spend; they had attempted distribution through app stores and carrier partnerships, but they completely lacked momentum because nothing they built made future user acquisition or retention easier, and they had no system that connected user feedback to product improvement.

INTEGRATION FAILURE

The execution unfolded in two phases, demonstrating that campaigns without systems collapse once marketing spend ceases to drive artificial growth. The first phase, April through June 2020, was the launch campaign, during which massive marketing spend generated initial awareness and trial. They activated 4.5 million free trials in the first months, received extensive press coverage, temporarily dominated app store charts, and sparked public debate over whether short-form premium content would succeed.

The marketing campaign worked in a narrow sense; it created awareness and drove downloads, but it lacked a mechanism to sustain growth once campaign spending normalized. Users who tried Quibi largely did not return: the content did not create habitual viewing behavior, the value proposition was not compelling enough to justify a $4.99 monthly subscription when competing against Netflix, YouTube, TikTok, and traditional streaming services, and the "mobile-only" restriction (later relaxed) meant content could not be watched on TVs where most streaming consumption happened.

The second phase, July through October 2020, tested whether the business could transition from campaign-driven growth to sustainable user acquisition and retention; the answer was a definitive no. As marketing spend normalized after the launch blitz, user acquisition collapsed. They were not building word-of-mouth or viral growth, and organic discovery was minimal.

Retention remained catastrophic, with fewer than 12% of free-trial users converting to paid subscriptions, meaning their customer lifetime value was a small fraction of their customer acquisition cost, even with massive marketing efficiency. They attempted product pivots, adding TV viewing after mobile-only restriction proved unpopular, exploring content bundling with other services, and testing international expansion. However, these were tactical adjustments that did not address the fundamental absence of a system connecting product, distribution, and retention. By October 2020, just 6 months after launching with $1.75 billion in funding and unprecedented media attention, Quibi announced it was shutting down and returning the remaining capital to investors.

💡 THE LESSON

Quibi's failure validates this chapter's central argument that systems beat campaigns and that having product, marketing, and distribution without integration leads to failure, even with unlimited resources. Analyzing through the systems lens reveals how each force was present but disconnected: they had velocity in content production and marketing execution but no feedback loop connecting user behavior to product iteration; they had distribution through app stores and carrier partnerships but no mechanism making distribution progressively more efficient; they attempted to create momentum through content library and celebrity talent but built nothing that made future growth easier or cheaper than past growth. Each new user was as expensive to acquire as the first, and retention never improved because product-market fit never materialized.

It also shows that in consumer businesses where retention determines unit economics, campaigns can generate initial awareness, but only systems create sustainable growth through compounding advantages. Most critically for founders, the three forces must integrate systematically. Velocity without feedback loops wastes resources on iterations that do not improve outcomes. Distribution without retention mechanisms converts marketing spend into churn rather than into customer base growth. Momentum requires building compounding advantages where early success makes future success easier, not just spending more money to maintain growth rates.

Key Takeaways

The argument developed in this chapter resolves into a handful of core points:

- Markets and organizations have natural rhythms and adoption curves that cannot be rushed without cost; premature scaling or forced transitions before solid foundations are established create problems that compound over time.
- Patient capital and disciplined resource allocation enable long-term advantage building by prioritizing investments that compound over time and reducing pressure to optimize for short-term metrics.
- At the same time, some market windows do exist in which moving fast captures opportunities that close, requiring an accurate assessment of which advantages are truly fleeting and which are durable.

Once systems replace campaigns, effort stops being the primary constraint. Many organizations find themselves surrounded by signals but slow to act on them. At that point, the problem is no longer how growth is organized, but how quickly information is translated into judgment and action. That question shapes what follows.

Chapter 8

Data, AI, and the Speed of Decisions

Data has no inherent value until it accelerates or improves decisions, requiring systems that translate information into faster learning and better choices rather than just creating dashboards.

— *Gartner Research, Decision Intelligence*

Data as Decision Accelerator

Data creates value only when it speeds up or improves decisions. Yet most startups drown in metrics while moving slowly to make decisions. They build elaborate dashboards that no one regularly reviews. They track hundreds of metrics without understanding which ones actually inform strategy. They collect enormous amounts of information without translating it into better or faster decisions. The result is the worst of both worlds: the organizational burden of maintaining data infrastructure without the benefits of faster learning and better decision-making.

The companies that create genuine competitive advantage through data do not have more data than their competitors. They have better systems for turning data into decisions quickly. They know precisely which questions they need to answer to make better strategic choices. They know which signals to trust and which to ignore. They know when to move fast based on incomplete information and when to wait for additional clarity. They understand that the goal is not perfect information, which does not exist, but sufficient information delivered quickly enough to maintain velocity and capitalize on opportunities before they close. If data is meant to accelerate decisions, the first question is not what to measure, but what decisions need to be made.

Building Data Infrastructure That Matters

The foundation of effective data usage is instrumentation that captures what matters without creating noise that obscures the signal. This requires starting with clarity about the fundamental questions the business needs to answer at each stage of its development. Early-stage companies need to understand whether they are building something people actually want, which means tracking engagement depth, retention curves, and qualitative feedback about the core value proposition. They need to understand which acquisition sources attract users who actually stick around, rather than just generate vanity metrics on total signups. They need to understand which actions or usage patterns predict long-term retention so they can optimize onboarding and activation flows accordingly.

As companies scale, the questions evolve, but the principle remains constant. Growth-stage companies need to understand unit economics at a granular level, tracking customer acquisition costs, lifetime value, and payback periods across segments and channels. They need to understand where they have pricing power and where they are competing primarily on price. They need to understand which features drive expansion revenue and which are table stakes that customers expect but do not pay more for. They need to understand their retention curves well enough to predict future revenue and to identify early warning signals when cohorts underperform expectations.

The mistake most companies make is instrumenting everything without prioritizing what matters most, creating systems that capture enormous amounts of data while failing to surface the specific insights that should drive behavior change. The better approach is to work backwards from decisions to instrumentation, identifying the choices you need to make well and then building data infrastructure specifically designed to inform those choices. This creates focus and ensures that the data you collect is actually used rather than accumulating in databases that no one queries.

Decision Rights and Data Access

One of the most important but least discussed aspects of using data effectively is ensuring that the people closest to decisions have direct access to the data they need without requiring permission or assistance from gatekeepers. When data access is centralized and controlled, and every question requires submitting a request to an analytics team with competing priorities, decision velocity slows dramatically, and the organization loses its ability to learn quickly from market feedback.

Modern data infrastructure enables broad access to data while maintaining appropriate security and privacy controls. Product managers should be able to query user behavior directly rather than waiting for weekly reports. Marketing teams should be able to view channel performance in real-time rather than relying on static dashboards. Sales leaders should be able to analyze pipeline conversion rates themselves rather than requesting custom reports. Customer success teams should be able to track account health metrics in real-time rather than relying on periodic reviews.

This democratization of data access requires investment in tools that make querying accessible to non-technical users, training to help teams understand which questions they can answer themselves, and cultural norms that encourage exploration and analysis. It requires accepting that people will sometimes draw incorrect conclusions from data they analyze themselves, while recognizing that the cost of occasional misinterpretation is lower than the cost of slow learning and delayed decisions arising from centralized data access.

The companies that move fastest are those in which data literacy is widespread, questioning assumptions with data is routine, and teams are empowered to make decisions based on what they see in the data without escalating every choice to senior leadership. This distributes decision-making to where information is freshest and most relevant, enabling the kind of velocity that creates compounding advantages over competitors who remain dependent on centralized analytics functions. At that point, speed itself becomes the constraint.

Decision Speed as Strategic Constraint

Speed in decision-making is important because markets evolve continuously and opportunities have limited windows. A decision made today with 80% confidence often creates more value than a decision made next month with 95% confidence, particularly in fast-moving markets where conditions change rapidly.

The opportunity cost of delayed decisions compounds over time as competitors move forward, market conditions evolve, and the strategic landscape shifts. Data should accelerate this process by providing rapid feedback on whether decisions are working, rather than creating analysis paralysis in which every choice requires exhaustive study before action. But speed alone is insufficient if it does not translate into faster learning.

Learning Speed Versus Prediction Accuracy

The most important contribution of data and AI to startup success is not prediction accuracy but learning speed. Startups operate in high-uncertainty environments where perfect prediction is impossible, and market conditions evolve faster than models can be updated. The advantage goes not to those who predict perfectly but to those who learn from errors quickly and adjust their approach before competitors recognize the change.

This suggests a fundamentally different approach to data science than what typically gets practiced in larger organizations. Large companies often optimize their models exhaustively, running numerous A/B tests and fine-tuning algorithms to extract marginal improvements in performance. They can afford to do so because they operate under relatively stable conditions, where small improvements in conversion rates or recommendation accuracy translate directly into significant revenue impact, given their scale. Startups operate in fundamentally different conditions: the market is still being defined, product-market fit is uncertain, and the greatest risks are not suboptimal conversion rates but building something nobody wants or missing market transitions entirely.

For startups, the goal is to build systems that quickly surface surprising information and make it easy to act on it. You want to know within days, not quarters, when a new acquisition channel is working better than expected or worse than projected. You want to know within weeks whether a new feature is driving the retention improvements you anticipated or whether users are ignoring it entirely. You want to know as soon as possible when a competitor launches something that changes customer expectations, or when a market trend creates new opportunities or threats.

This emphasis on speed over precision has implications for how data teams and analytics infrastructure are built. Small, embedded analysts who work directly with product, marketing, and sales teams create more value than large centralized data science teams that produce sophisticated models but remain distant from actual decision-making. Simple dashboards that surface key metrics in real-time create more value than elaborate reports that take weeks to produce. Automated alerts that flag unusual patterns create more value than scheduled review meetings where data gets presented but not acted upon. Over time, this difference in learning speed compounds into a structural advantage.

Building Competitive Advantage Through Data

Data creates sustainable competitive advantage not through any single insight but through accumulated learning embedded in products, strategy, and operations, making it increasingly difficult for competitors to replicate. Companies like Amazon, Netflix, and Google have built enormous moats not because they have more data than competitors, though they often do, but because they have built organizational systems that turn data into better decisions faster than anyone else in their markets.

This kind of advantage compounds over time as the gap between leaders and followers widens. Better data leads to better decisions, which lead to better outcomes, which generate more customers, which generate more data, which enable even better decisions. The cycle reinforces itself as long as the company maintains the infrastructure and culture that enables fast learning. Breaking into markets dominated by incumbents with sophisticated data advantages becomes progressively harder, not because their products are necessarily superior, but because they can optimize and adapt more quickly.

Building this kind of advantage requires treating data as a strategic asset that warrants sustained investment, even when the return is not immediately apparent. It requires hiring people who can translate between data and strategy, who understand both the technical capabilities of data systems and the business context that makes certain insights valuable. It requires building infrastructure that scales with the business rather than requiring constant rebuilding. It requires resisting the temptation to use data primarily for reporting to investors or boards rather than for improving the business. Once decision systems exist, the next question becomes how much of this work can be accelerated further.

AI as Leverage, Not Theater

Artificial intelligence has become both overhyped and underutilized in the startup ecosystem. Companies feel pressure to incorporate AI into their products and operations, often without clear thinking about where it actually creates value versus where it is primarily theater designed to appeal to investors or generate press coverage. The question is not whether to use AI but where AI actually accelerates learning, improves decisions, or creates genuine customer value that was previously impossible or impractical.

AI creates legitimate value in several specific contexts that startups can leverage without requiring massive research teams or computational resources. Personalization at scale becomes practical with machine learning models that tailor experiences to individual users based on behavioral patterns, enabling customization that would be impossible with manual rules or segmentation. Customer service and support can be augmented with AI systems that handle routine questions and triage complex issues to humans, improving response times while reducing costs. Sales and marketing can use predictive models to identify high-probability prospects, optimize messaging, and forecast revenue with greater accuracy than traditional methods.

The key is to distinguish between AI as genuine leverage and AI as a superficial feature that adds complexity without commensurate value. Genuine leverage means using AI to perform tasks that were previously impossible or prohibitively expensive, creating step-function improvements in capability or cost. Superficial features are those where AI produces incrementally better results than simpler approaches, but at costs that do not justify the improvement, or worse, where AI is used primarily for positioning rather than because it actually solves customer problems better.

AI, Data, and Structural Lock-In

As AI capabilities become more accessible and democratized through cloud services and open-source tools, the question of whether AI can create a lasting competitive advantage becomes more nuanced. Access to AI technology itself is not a moat when everyone can use similar models and tools. The moat derives from proprietary data that improves your models for your specific use case, from organizational capabilities that enable effective AI deployment, and from product architectures that create feedback loops in which AI improves automatically as more users engage with the product.

Companies that build genuine AI advantages do so by creating systems in which their AI improves through use in ways that competitors cannot easily replicate. Recommendation engines improve as more users interact with them, creating better experiences that drive greater usage and generate more training data. Computer vision models improve as more images are processed and labeled, yielding accuracy gains that compound over time. Natural language processing improves as more conversations get processed, creating more natural interactions that drive adoption.

The strategic question for startups is not whether to use AI, but whether they can create the kind of data feedback loops that turn AI into a genuine moat rather than merely a feature competitors can match. This often requires rethinking product architecture from the ground up to enable these feedback loops rather than bolting AI onto existing products as an afterthought. It requires patience to let the advantage compound over time rather than expecting immediate differentiation.

Maintaining Human Judgment

Despite the increasing sophistication of data systems and AI capabilities, human judgment remains essential in navigating the ambiguity and novelty that characterize startup environments. Data tells you what happened and can predict what might happen based on historical patterns, but it cannot tell you what you should do when facing genuinely new situations where historical patterns do not apply. AI can optimize within existing paradigms but struggles with the kind of creative problem-solving required when those paradigms themselves must change.

The most effective organizations use data and AI to augment, rather than replace, human judgment, creating systems in which humans focus on decisions that require creativity, empathy, and strategic thinking, while delegating routine pattern-matching and optimization to automated systems. Customer service representatives address complex emotional situations, whereas chatbots address routine questions. Product managers make strategic decisions about what to build while algorithms optimize the details of how features get presented. Salespeople focus on relationship-building and complex negotiations, whereas AI systems handle lead scoring and forecasting.

This division of labor requires careful consideration of which decisions benefit from automation and which require human judgment. It requires building systems that make it easy for humans to override automated decisions when context suggests the algorithm is missing something important. It requires creating feedback loops in which humans override the algorithms to improve them over time, rather than treating them as exceptions to ignore.

The companies that will thrive in an AI-enabled world are not those that automate everything possible but those that find the right balance between automated systems and human judgment, leveraging each where it creates the most value. Data and AI are tools that accelerate learning and improve decisions when used thoughtfully, but they are not substitutes for the hard work of understanding your market, building products people want, and executing with discipline.The goal is not to eliminate human decision-making but to make those decisions better informed and faster, thereby creating the velocity that yields sustainable competitive advantage.

🔍 *Case Study - Gojek*

When Decision Velocity Becomes Competitive Moat

In 2010, when Nadiem Makarim founded Gojek in Jakarta, Indonesia, the business began as a simple call center connecting motorcycle taxi drivers, known locally as "ojek," with customers seeking rides through the city's notoriously congested streets. Indonesia's transportation infrastructure created perfect conditions for motorcycle taxis: traffic gridlock made cars impractical for short trips, public transportation was limited and unreliable, millions of motorcycle owners needed supplemental income, and the country's archipelagic geography with limited road infrastructure made two-wheeled transportation essential.

Yet, the initial model had severe limitations: call center operations could not efficiently match riders with drivers at scale; pricing was negotiated inconsistently; quality control was nearly impossible; and geographic expansion required proportional growth in call center staff. The transformation came when Makarim rebuilt Gojek as a mobile platform in 2015, leveraging accelerating smartphone adoption across Southeast Asia to create a digital marketplace connecting drivers and riders. This shift from call center to platform was necessary but insufficient. The real competitive advantage emerged when Gojek recognized that managing millions of daily micro-decisions across expanding service offerings required data infrastructure and algorithmic decision systems that operated at a speed impossible for human judgment.

DATA AS DECISION INFRASTRUCTURE

Gojek's evolution demonstrated how data and AI create competitive advantage not through prediction theater or futuristic capabilities but through dramatically accelerating decision velocity while maintaining or improving decision quality. The first critical system involved dynamic driver allocation, matching incoming ride requests with available drivers based on proximity, traffic conditions, driver ratings, estimated pickup times, and predicted demand patterns.

This was not about revolutionary data or AI technology. The underlying algorithms relied on relatively straightforward optimization techniques. The true competitive advantage lay in execution: the ability to compute allocation decisions in under one second for every ride request, at massive scale, processing millions of requests each day across dozens of cities in Indonesia. Human dispatchers could not match this decision velocity, and competitors without comparable data infrastructure either made slower allocation decisions that led to longer wait times and lower driver utilization, or made faster but lower-quality decisions that hurt customer experience and driver earnings.

The second data system focused on dynamic pricing that balanced supply and demand in real-time while maintaining customer trust and regulatory compliance. Southeast Asian ride-hailing markets were highly price-sensitive, making surge pricing politically and commercially risky. Yet, efficient markets require price signals that attract drivers during high-demand periods and discourage frivolous requests during periods of supply constraint.

Gojek's pricing algorithms adjusted fares based on real-time supply-demand balance, predicted wait times, traffic conditions, weather patterns, and local events, making thousands of pricing decisions per minute across different service types and geographic zones. The AI value was not in perfect price prediction but in decision velocity. They could test pricing changes, measure customer and driver responses, and continuously adjust algorithms, iterating toward optimal pricing far faster than competitors using manual pricing rules or slower algorithmic systems.

The third critical system involved fraud detection and trust mechanisms that enabled platform growth while managing risk posed by bad actors on both the supply and demand sides. With millions of transactions daily and expansion into financial services through GoPay, Gojek faced fraud attempts ranging from driver account manipulation to payment fraud to the generation of fake transactions.

Their machine learning systems analyzed transaction patterns, device fingerprints, behavioral signals, and network relationships to flag suspicious activity in real-time, blocking fraudulent transactions before they are completed while minimizing false positives that could harm legitimate users. Again, the competitive advantage was not technological sophistication; many fraud detection techniques were standard, but execution velocity: they could detect and respond to emerging fraud patterns within hours rather than weeks, preventing fraud losses while maintaining a seamless experience for legitimate users.

EXPANSION THROUGH DECISION VELOCITY

The execution unfolded across three phases, demonstrating how data infrastructure, which enables faster, better decisions, became the foundation for the expansion of the multi-service super-app. The first phase, 2015 through 2017, focused on establishing ride-hailing dominance in Indonesia and building data infrastructure to support additional services. They expanded from Jakarta to cities across Java and to other Indonesian islands, achieving market leadership through superior driver allocation that reduced wait times, dynamic pricing that maintained affordability while ensuring driver supply, and fraud detection that built trust in digital transactions.

During this period, their investment in data infrastructure created compounding advantages: more rides generated more data that improved allocation algorithms, which attracted more drivers and riders, which generated more data in a virtuous cycle. Competitors like Grab (which had acquired Uber's Southeast Asian operations) had comparable technology, but Gojek's Indonesia-specific data density and decision velocity gave them an edge in local markets where they competed directly.

The second phase, 2017 through 2019, tested whether the data infrastructure built for ride-hailing could accelerate expansion into adjacent services that required similar real-time decision-making at scale. They launched GoFood, a food delivery service that required managing restaurant partnerships, optimizing delivery routes, and forecasting demand. They expanded GoPay from a ride payment method to a standalone digital wallet, requiring fraud detection, merchant acquisition, and regulatory compliance.

They added GoSend for package delivery, GoMart for grocery delivery, GoMed for pharmacy delivery, and eventually expanded to 20+ services, ranging from massage booking to professional cleaning to video streaming. Each service required millions of daily micro-decisions, such as which delivery driver to assign to which restaurant order, which route to optimize for multiple package pickups, how to price instant delivery versus scheduled delivery, and when to predict demand spikes that require driver pre-positioning. Gojek's data infrastructure enabled launching and scaling these services far faster than competitors, and it built decision systems from scratch for each vertical.

The third phase began around 2019 when Gojek's super-app strategy demonstrated that decision velocity created a strategic moat beyond individual service quality. They processed over 2 billion transactions annually across all services, making them one of Indonesia's largest transaction platforms. Their GoPay wallet had become the preferred payment method for millions of users, creating a financial services moat beyond transportation.

Most critically, their data infrastructure meant that launching new services primarily required product and operational execution. The underlying decision systems for allocation, pricing, fraud detection, and demand forecasting were largely reusable across verticals, with vertical-specific tuning. This gave Gojek a structural advantage in the super-app race: they could expand into new services faster than single-service competitors could match their breadth, and they could operate a multi-service platform more efficiently than competitors without comparable data infrastructure because their systems made millions of optimizing decisions automatically.

In 2021, Gojek merged with Tokopedia, Indonesia's largest e-commerce platform, forming GoTo Group, which went public in 2022 with an initial valuation exceeding $30 billion despite challenging public market conditions.

💡 THE LESSON

Gojek's trajectory validates that AI and data create competitive advantage through decision velocity rather than prediction accuracy or technological sophistication, and that organizations that can make better decisions faster than competitors compound advantages across multiple business lines. Analyzing through the data and AI lens reveals how decision systems amplified all three forces: velocity improved because they could launch new services and iterate algorithms far faster than competitors building decision systems from scratch; momentum compounded because data from each service improved systems that benefited all services, creating flywheel where scale begat better decisions which drove more scale; and distribution became more efficient because better allocation and pricing meant higher customer satisfaction and driver earnings, reducing acquisition costs through word-of-mouth and retention.

In platform businesses that require millions of real-time decisions, data infrastructure becomes the business moat, not through futuristic AI capabilities, but by enabling decision velocity that competitors cannot match without comparable investment and data density. Most critically for founders, Gojek illustrates that AI's value lies in operational leverage: their data scientists did not need to predict the future or replace human judgment, but they built systems that made allocation, pricing, fraud detection, and forecasting decisions orders of magnitude faster than humans while maintaining decision quality, and this velocity advantage compounded across every service vertical they entered.

Key Takeaways

Viewed as a system rather than a set of tools, the implications of data-driven decision-making become difficult to ignore.

- Effective data infrastructure starts with clarity about which questions the business needs to answer, rather than instrumenting everything and hoping insights emerge.
- Speed of decision-making matters because market opportunities have limited windows. Most companies slow themselves down by confusing data collection with decision acceleration.
- AI and automation should be deployed primarily to increase the velocity of learning and execution rather than to replace human judgment on strategic questions.

As decisions accelerate, the question quietly changes. The bottleneck is no longer insight, infrastructure, or even judgment, but the collective ability of a group to move in the same direction at the same time. How that coherence is created and sustained as complexity grows is the focus of the next chapter.

Chapter 9:

Teams That Create Momentum

Organizations that sustain momentum are not those
with the most people or resources but those with
talent density, strategic alignment, and cultures
where learning from failure is valued more than
avoiding mistakes.

— Reed Hastings, No Rules Rules

Founder-led Growth in the Beginning

In the earliest stages of a startup, growth cannot be delegated to specialists because the company is still determining what works and why. The founder must be directly involved in growth efforts, not merely to reduce hiring costs, but because the learning that comes from engaging directly with customers, channels, and messaging is essential to developing the strategic understanding that will guide all future scaling efforts. Founders who delegate growth too early, before they fully understand their own growth dynamics, create organizations that lack strategic clarity about how the business operates.

This direct involvement entails founders undertaking tasks that seem beneath their role or outside their expertise. It means writing their own early content rather than hiring content marketers. It means running the first paid advertising campaigns themselves rather than engaging agencies. It entails making sales calls rather than hiring salespeople. This hands-on work is not about cost savings. It is about developing the pattern recognition and intuition that only comes from direct experience with what works and what does not in your specific market with your specific product.

Brian Chesky of Airbnb personally photographed listings in New York in the early days, not because Airbnb could not afford photographers but because he needed to understand intimately what made listings successful and what prevented guests from booking. That understanding informed product decisions, quality standards, and eventually the entire operational playbook for how Airbnb would scale. If he had delegated that work immediately, he would have lost the direct feedback loop that shaped his understanding of the business.

The transition from founder-led to team-led growth is one of the most difficult and important challenges a startup faces. Move too slowly, and you constrain growth to what the founder can personally execute. Move too quickly, and you hire people to execute on strategies that have not been validated, wasting money and time while creating organizational complexity that slows learning. The right moment to transition is when the founder can clearly articulate what works and why, and can teach someone else the playbook rather than delegating responsibility and hoping the new hire figures it out.

Alignment Over Organizational Structure

Most startups organize themselves along conventional functional divisions, creating separate teams for product, marketing, and sales that report through distinct lines of authority to leadership. This structure seems natural and is how most companies operate, but it systematically creates misalignment on the questions that matter most for growth. Product teams optimize for features and user experience without sufficient consideration for how those choices affect marketing and sales. Marketing teams create campaigns and messaging that do not fully leverage product capabilities or reflect product roadmaps. Sales teams promise capabilities or roadmap commitments that do not align with product priorities.

The result is friction and inefficiency that becomes more pronounced as the company scales. Product launches for which marketing and sales are not prepared to provide support. Marketing campaigns that highlight features customers do not care about or that are not differentiated relative to competitors. Sales processes that do not align with how the product is designed for sale. Each function hits its local objectives while the overall growth system remains suboptimal.

The alternative is to organize around growth itself as the primary objective, with product, marketing, and sales understood as interconnected components of a unified system rather than as independent functions. This does not necessarily mean eliminating functional specialization or creating matrix organizations with complex reporting structures. It means creating mechanisms that compel alignment on the questions that matter most: whom we are targeting, what value we deliver, how we position ourselves, what our growth model is, and how each function supports that model.

Companies that achieve this alignment often do so through cross-functional teams that own growth outcomes end-to-end rather than through traditional functional divisions. A growth team might include product managers, engineers, designers, marketers, and data analysts, all working together to increase activation rates or improve retention in a specific segment. The team owns the entire problem and is evaluated on outcomes rather than on functional metrics such as features shipped or leads generated.

Stripe organized much of its early growth efforts around cross-functional squads that owned specific user journeys or market segments end to end. A team focused on developer adoption included engineers building API tools, technical writers creating documentation, developer advocates creating content and engaging with communities, and product managers ensuring the entire experience was coherent. This structure created natural alignment because everyone on the team understood that they succeeded or failed together based on developer adoption, rather than on whether they met their individual functional metrics.

Talent Density Over Headcount

One of the most persistent mistakes in scaling startups is believing that growth problems can be solved primarily by adding headcount, that more people automatically create more capacity and therefore more growth. In reality, adding people too quickly often slows growth rather than accelerating it, creating communication overhead, coordination costs, and cultural dilution that outweigh the additional capacity.

The companies that scale most effectively focus on talent density rather than headcount growth, hiring exceptional people who can operate with high degrees of autonomy and judgment rather than hiring adequate people who need extensive management and direction. One exceptional product manager who can own an entire problem space creates more value than three adequate product managers who need constant coordination and oversight. One exceptional engineer who can architect systems and mentor others creates more value than five mediocre engineers who produce code but not sustainable systems.

This focus on talent density requires the willingness to pay premium compensation for exceptional individuals rather than attempting to maximize headcount within budget constraints. It requires being patient in hiring, waiting for candidates who clearly raise the bar rather than filling positions quickly with merely acceptable candidates. It requires being ruthless about performance management, moving quickly when people are not performing, rather than retaining low performers because you are hesitant to have difficult conversations.

Netflix articulated this philosophy explicitly in its culture document, emphasizing that it seeks to be a professional sports team, with every position filled by an excellent performer, rather than a family in which everyone is tolerated regardless of performance. This may sound harsh, but it creates organizations in which people can operate with high trust and minimal process, because everyone is confident that their colleagues will perform well without constant supervision.

The practical implication is that founders should resist pressure to rapidly scale headcount, even when capital is available. The right pace of hiring is determined by your ability to maintain culture and quality, not by how much money you have raised. Hiring ahead of validated need creates organizations full of people looking for work, which leads to the creation of work projects, internal politics, and a loss of focus on what actually matters.

Building Institutional Capabilities

As organizations grow beyond the point where individual excellence alone can carry execution, they must convert people-dependent strengths into repeatable systems. This transition requires transforming the tacit knowledge held by founders and early employees into explicit systems, processes, and playbooks that others can execute.

This codification is difficult because much of what makes early teams successful is intuition and judgment that has developed through experience, but is hard to articulate explicitly. Founders often know their product and market well enough to make sound decisions quickly, even though they cannot explain precisely how they reached their conclusions. Early marketers know what messaging resonates through trial and error, but struggle to articulate the underlying principles that make some messages work, and others fail.

Building institutional capabilities entails the hard work of making tacit knowledge explicit. It means writing down the sales playbook that exists informally in how the founder sells. It means documenting the customer insights that inform product decisions. It means creating frameworks and principles that help new hires understand how to make decisions in ambiguous situations. It entails developing onboarding processes that transfer knowledge efficiently rather than requiring every new hire to relearn everything through experience.

Companies that do this well create tremendous leverage because they can scale without losing the judgment and understanding that made them successful initially. New product managers understand customer needs more deeply because they rely on documented insights and research rather than institutional folklore. New marketers understand positioning because there are clear frameworks rather than just examples of past campaigns. New salespeople ramp quickly because there are playbooks rather than just tribal knowledge.

Maintaining Velocity at Scale

The central challenge of scaling teams is maintaining the velocity that characterized the early stages as the organization grows and becomes more complex. Every new person adds communication overhead. Every new team creates coordination needs. Every layer of management adds decision latency. These forces naturally slow organizations down unless you actively fight them.

Maintaining velocity requires several disciplines that feel unnatural as companies grow. It requires keeping teams small even as the company grows, resisting the temptation to add people to teams simply because you have budget or because people want management opportunities. It requires preserving decision authority at the edge rather than centralizing decisions as the organization grows. It requires maintaining direct communication across functions rather than allowing information to flow only through management layers. It requires continuously investing in infrastructure and tools that reduce friction, even when those investments have uncertain ROI.

Amazon's two-pizza team rule embodies this principle, keeping teams small enough to be fed by two pizzas and ensuring that each team has sufficient autonomy to move quickly without constant coordination. Spotify's squad structure serves a similar purpose, creating small cross-functional teams that own problems end-to-end rather than large functional organizations that require constant synchronization.

The test of whether you are maintaining velocity is not whether things feel comfortable but whether you can still ship quickly, learn fast, and adapt to market changes as rapidly as you did in earlier stages. If decisions that used to take days now take weeks, if launches that used to require one meeting now require five, if experiments that you used to run constantly now require extensive approval processes, you are losing velocity and need to actively simplify your organization.

Culture as Competitive Advantage

Over time, the behaviors that preserve or destroy velocity become cultural rather than procedural. The teams that create sustainable momentum build cultures in which the behaviors that drive growth are natural and self-reinforcing, rather than requiring constant management intervention. In these cultures, people are biased toward action rather than analysis paralysis. They share information openly rather than hoarding it for political advantage. They focus on customers rather than internal dynamics. They experiment constantly rather than trying to plan perfectly. They give honest feedback rather than avoiding difficult conversations.

Building this kind of culture is not about having better values or mission statements than competitors. Every company claims to value innovation, customer focus, and collaboration. Culture is determined by which behaviors are rewarded, which mistakes are punished, and which trade-offs are made when values conflict. If you say you value speed but reward extensive planning, people will plan extensively. If you say you value honesty but punish people who surface problems, people will hide problems. If you say you value customers but measure teams on features shipped rather than on customer outcomes, teams will optimize for feature delivery.

Creating cultures that drive momentum requires being deliberate about what behaviors you reward and being willing to make hiring and firing decisions based on cultural fit, even when individuals are otherwise talented. It requires founders and leaders to model the behaviors they want to see rather than just talking about them. It requires early detection and correction of cultural drift before it becomes entrenched. It requires accepting that strong cultures necessarily exclude some people who might be talented but do not fit the specific behaviors your company needs to succeed.

The companies that build truly great teams understand that hiring is just the beginning. The real work is creating an environment in which talented people can do the best work of their careers, where they have the autonomy to make decisions, the information they need to make sound decisions, the trust to take risks without fear, and the feedback to improve continuously. Teams that create momentum are not those with the most resources or the most impressive credentials. They are those that have built the capabilities, alignment, and culture that enable them to execute with unusual velocity and learn from their market faster than anyone else. This is where sustainable competitive advantage originates.

These principles become most visible when organizational structure is treated not as an administrative choice, but as a growth lever in its own right. The difference between teams that stall and teams that compound often lies less in strategy than in how people are organized to execute it.

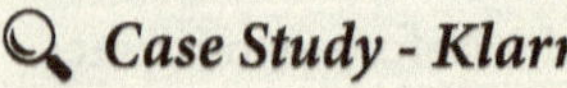
Case Study - Klarna

When Organizational Structure Amplifies the Three Forces

When Sebastian Siemiatkowski, Niklas Adalberth, and Victor Jacobsson founded Klarna in Stockholm in 2005, they entered the e-commerce payments market with a clear conviction: organizational structure would determine whether product innovation could evolve into a durable competitive advantage. Their founding vision centered on eliminating checkout friction. At the time, European e-commerce suffered from low conversion rates because customers had to enter payment details before fully engaging with products, were reluctant to share credit card information with unfamiliar merchants, and faced complex checkout flows that often led to cart abandonment.

Klarna's initial product innovation, "buy now, pay later," allowed customers to receive products before paying and effectively addressed these friction points. But the founders recognized that product innovation alone would not sustain leadership as competitors copied features. The companies that would win would be those whose organizational structure accelerated learning velocity, aligned teams around outcomes rather than activities, and maintained talent density that multiplied individual contributions rather than diluting them through bureaucratic headcount growth.

FOUNDER-LED GROWTH CULTURE

Klarna's approach demonstrated how organizational design either amplifies or dampens the three forces that create sustainable growth. The first structural principle was maintaining a founder-led culture even as the company scaled from a startup to a public company serving 150 million users across 45 countries. Sebastian Siemiatkowski remained CEO through all growth phases, providing continuity of vision and decision-making authority that prevented the strategic drift common when professional managers replace founders before product-market fit fully matures across markets.

This was not founder ego but a structural advantage: Siemiatkowski's direct involvement in product decisions, merchant partnerships, and market expansion ensured strategic choices remained aligned with the original vision of reducing checkout friction and improving consumer purchasing power, even as tactics evolved across different markets and business models. Companies that transitioned to professional management earlier often lost this strategic coherence, with new executives optimizing for different metrics or pursuing adjacent markets that diluted focus.

The second organizational principle focused on aligning product, engineering, and marketing around a single North Star metric: repeat usage, rather than allowing functional siloes to optimize for conflicting objectives. Traditional organizational structures created misalignment: product teams optimized for feature completeness, engineering teams prioritized technical architecture, marketing teams focused on new customer acquisition, and these different optimization targets often conflicted.

Klarna structured cross-functional "squads" that owned specific customer outcomes, such as "first-time purchase conversion" or "repeat usage within 30 days," with each squad containing product managers, engineers, designers, and growth specialists collectively responsible for improving their metric. This alignment meant every team member understood how their work connected to business outcomes, reduced coordination overhead by having decisions happen within squads rather than across functional hierarchies, and created accountability so teams could not blame other functions for failing to hit targets.

The third structural principle emphasized talent density over headcount growth, recognizing that in technology businesses, exceptional individuals create disproportionate value and that maintaining a high performance bar as the organization scales matters more than adding bodies to handle growing complexity. They practiced selective hiring, leaving positions unfilled rather than compromising on talent quality; compensated top performers at levels that retained them despite competitive pressure; and deliberately kept teams smaller than industry norms to maintain communication efficiency and individual accountability.

This talent density created multiplicative effects: exceptional engineers built more maintainable systems that reduced future technical debt, strong product managers made better trade-off decisions that avoided costly pivots, and high-performing growth marketers achieved higher customer acquisition efficiency, reducing burn rate. Companies that prioritized headcount growth to "scale the team" often created organizational complexity that reduced productivity per person faster than additional people increased total output.

ALIGNMENT OVER HIERARCHY

The execution unfolded across three phases that demonstrated how organizational structure amplified competitive advantages as the business scaled. The first phase, 2005 through 2014, established the foundational organizational principles while building product-market fit in Nordic markets. They maintained a flat hierarchy where individual contributors had direct access to leadership, made decisions based on data and customer feedback rather than institutional politics, and iterated rapidly on product features because small teams could coordinate without extensive approval processes.

During this period, their organizational velocity gave them an advantage over traditional payment companies with hierarchical structures. They could launch new features in weeks rather than quarters, test merchant partnerships and reverse course quickly if results disappointed, and maintain customer obsession because everyone from engineers to executives regularly interacted with merchant and consumer feedback. This velocity translated directly into competitive momentum: they captured the Nordic buy-now-pay-later market before competitors recognized the opportunity, built merchant relationships that created switching costs, and established brand recognition that made expansion into adjacent markets easier.

The second phase, 2014 through 2019, tested whether organizational principles that worked at startup scale could maintain velocity as headcount grew from hundreds to thousands of employees and geographic presence expanded from the Nordic region to the US, UK, Germany, Australia, and eventually 45 countries. Many companies experience "scale drag," where organizational complexity slows decision-making, bureaucracy replaces judgment, and political considerations override customer needs.

Klarna maintained velocity through structural choices: they preserved squad-based organization where small cross-functional teams owned outcomes rather than creating functional hierarchies where product, engineering, and marketing operated separately; they kept Siemiatkowski directly involved in strategic decisions rather than adding management layers that filtered information; they continued prioritizing talent density by maintaining high hiring bar even when growth pressures tempted lower standards; and they invested in data infrastructure that provided squad-level visibility into customer behavior, enabling teams to make decisions based on evidence rather than escalating choices through management hierarchy.

The third phase began around 2019, when Klarna's organizational structure demonstrated a strategic moat amid intensifying competition from both fintech startups and traditional financial institutions launching buy-now-pay-later products. The competitive landscape included Afterpay (later acquired by Block for $29 billion), Affirm (founded by PayPal co-founder Max Levchin), PayPal's own BNPL offering, and dozens of regional competitors, yet Klarna maintained market leadership through organizational advantages: their squad structure enabled faster product iteration as consumer preferences shifted, their talent density meant they could enter new markets with smaller teams that moved faster than competitors' larger operations, and their founder-led culture maintained strategic coherence as they expanded from pure BNPL into broader consumer shopping and financial services.

By 2021, Klarna had reached 150 million active users, processed $80+ billion in annual payment volume, partnered with 400,000+ merchants, and achieved $45.6 billion private market valuation. This growth reflected organizational structure that amplified rather than dampened the three forces: velocity remained high because squad-based teams could iterate independently without coordination overhead; momentum compounded because repeat usage focus meant every product decision optimized for retention, creating flywheel where satisfied users returned and recommended Klarna to friends; and distribution efficiency improved because alignment between product and growth teams meant features like one-click checkout and in-app shopping served both user experience and merchant acquisition objectives.

💡 THE LESSON

Klarna's trajectory validates this chapter's central argument that organizational structure either amplifies or dampens the three forces that create sustainable growth, and that alignment matters more than hierarchy when building momentum. Analyzing through the organizational lens reveals how structural choices accelerated growth: founder-led culture maintained strategic coherence across markets and business model evolution; squad-based organization aligned cross-functional teams around outcomes rather than functional metrics, reducing coordination costs and improving decision quality; and talent density over headcount meant each employee created more value, maintaining velocity as complexity increased rather than experiencing typical scale drag where organizational growth reduces productivity per person.

The case demonstrates that in technology businesses where learning speed and iteration velocity determine competitive outcomes, organizational structure becomes a strategic weapon rather than an administrative detail.

For founders, Klarna illustrates that scaling successfully requires deliberately designing an organizational structure that preserves startup advantages, like decision speed, customer obsession, and outcome accountability. This is a better approach than defaulting to hierarchical models that may work for mature companies but stifle innovation and reduce velocity in growth-stage businesses where market leadership remains contested.

Key Takeaways

Based on the foregoing, how momentum is created inside teams as complexity grows is described by these patterns:

- Founder-led execution delivers unmatched early velocity because decisions are fast and context is complete, but scaling requires deliberately replacing that centrality with systems that preserve speed and momentum as complexity grows.
- Talent density matters more than headcount: small groups of exceptional people, operating with autonomy and shared context, outperform larger teams burdened by coordination, process, and managerial overhead.
- Momentum compounds when product, marketing, and sales are aligned around the same priorities, and culture functions as an execution system, distributing decision-making authority without fragmenting strategy.

When momentum is sustained, it no longer depends on individual heroics or constant intervention. The challenge shifts from moving faster to deciding what to protect, what to sacrifice, and what is allowed to compound over time.

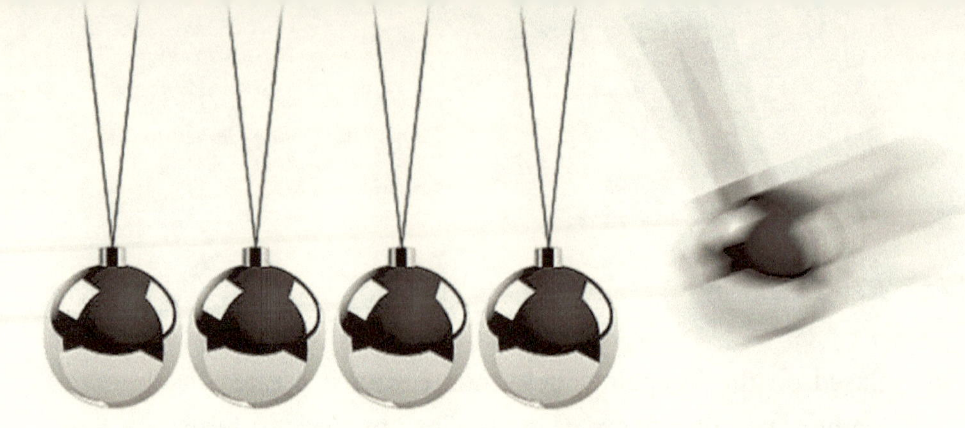

Chapter 10:

Playing the Long Game

Greatness is not achieved suddenly but built deliberately through countless decisions that prioritize what compounds over what merely impresses in the moment.

— *James Clear, Atomic Habits*

The Tyranny of Quarterly Thinking

Modern startups operate under intense pressure to demonstrate growth every quarter, meet arbitrary milestones that satisfy investors, maintain the momentum perception that drives subsequent funding rounds, and achieve growth rates that support ever-increasing valuations. This pressure creates systematic distortions in decision-making, incentivizing choices that prioritize short-term metrics over long-term value creation. Companies pull revenue forward through aggressive discounting. They invest in paid acquisition channels with poor unit economics but yield immediate growth. They optimize for the signals that investors track rather than the fundamentals that actually matter for building sustainable businesses.

The consequence is that many startups that appear successful on commonly tracked metrics are actually accumulating hidden liabilities that will eventually constrain or destroy their growth. They acquire customers at unsustainable costs who churn quickly once discounts expire. They develop products that users try but do not adopt enough to incorporate into routine workflows. They create revenue that is fundamentally transactional rather than recurring, requiring constant effort to maintain rather than compounding naturally. They optimize for vanity metrics that look impressive in pitch decks but do not translate into profitable, sustainable businesses.

The alternative is playing the long game, which means making decisions that optimize for building compounding advantages rather than hitting next quarter's numbers. It means being willing to invest in distribution channels that take years to mature, rather than in channels that yield immediate results. It means prioritizing retention over acquisition when resources are constrained, because retained customers compound, whereas acquired customers who churn do not. It means building products that solve important problems in depth rather than merely surface solutions to many problems. It means sometimes accepting slower visible growth to build stronger foundations that enable faster, sustainable growth later.

Compounding as a Strategic Framework

The single most important concept for playing the long game successfully is understanding compounding and structuring your business to maximize compounding effects. Compounding is what transforms linear efforts into exponential results, what creates value that accumulates over time rather than requiring constant renewal, what builds competitive advantages that become progressively harder to overcome. Companies that structure themselves around compounding create fundamentally different trajectories than companies focused on linear metrics.

Compounding requires identifying the elements of your business that can strengthen rather than weaken as they scale. Among these, distribution is often the most powerful, because it determines whether every other advantage can actually reach the market. Network effects compound as each additional user makes the product more valuable for all existing users, creating ever stronger incentives to join and remain on the platform.

Content libraries compound as more content gets added, making the platform more valuable and attracting more users who create more content. Brand compounds as more people encounter the company and form positive associations with it, making future marketing more efficient and enabling premium pricing. Data compounds: as usage increases, it generates more information that improves the product, which, in turn, drives even more usage. Distribution partnerships compound as relationships deepen and partners invest more in the relationship.

The strategic implication is that you should invest disproportionately in the elements of your business that compound rather than spreading resources evenly across all activities. If content compounds for your business, you should invest heavily in content, even if the immediate return is unclear. If brand compounds, you should invest in brand building, even though brand impact is difficult to measure precisely. If network effects compound, you should be willing to subsidize growth substantially in the early stages to reach the scale at which network effects become self-sustaining.

Scaling Without Losing Velocity

One of the great challenges of building enduring companies is maintaining the velocity that characterized early stages even as the organization grows larger and more complex. At this stage, velocity is no longer something to create, but something to defend against organizational drag. The natural tendency of organizations is to slow down as they scale, adding process, hierarchy, and coordination requirements that create friction and delay. The exceptional companies actively counter this tendency, treating velocity as an asset to protect rather than a luxury to sacrifice.

Maintaining velocity at scale requires deliberate architectural choices in how the organization is structured. It requires keeping teams small and sufficiently autonomous that they can make decisions and deliver quickly without requiring coordination across large groups. It requires maintaining flat organizational structures where information flows directly rather than through multiple management layers. It requires preserving direct customer contact for people building products rather than insulating them behind layers of process and intermediaries. It requires investing in tools and infrastructure that reduce friction even when the ROI is difficult to quantify precisely.

Amazon's approach to maintaining velocity is instructive. They structure teams to be as independent as possible, with each team owning specific services or product areas end-to-end. Teams have their own APIs and infrastructure, which creates some duplication but allows them to move quickly without coordinating changes across multiple teams. They prefer disaggregated services to shared services that create dependencies. They accept some level of chaos and duplication as the cost of maintaining velocity, recognizing that perfect coordination and efficiency often mean slow execution.

The test of whether you are successfully maintaining velocity is whether the pace of shipping, learning, and adaptation remains high relative to the organization's size. Larger organizations should ship more experiments and features than smaller organizations, not fewer. They should learn faster, not slower, because they have more resources and data. If your rate of progress is declining as your team grows, you are trading velocity for size, and that trade will eventually undermine your competitive position.

Protecting Momentum Through Transitions

Momentum is fragile, particularly during the major transitions that companies experience as they scale. Transitions create uncertainty, distraction, and often conflict as the organization adapts to new ways of operating. The transition from founder-led product to product management organization often loses the strong customer intuition that made the early product successful. The transition from founder-led sales to a sales organization often erodes the consultative selling approach and product expertise that enabled early deal closings.

Protecting momentum through these transitions requires careful consideration of what is changing and what must remain constant. The mechanisms might need to evolve, but the underlying principles and culture should persist. If founder-led selling succeeded because of deep product expertise and a consultative approach, then the sales organization must be built to replicate that rather than importing conventional sales playbooks. If early products succeeded because of tight customer feedback loops, then the product organization must preserve those loops even as it scales.

This often means hiring non-traditional people who can operate in your specific context, rather than hiring people with impressive credentials from larger companies who expect to operate as they did in their previous environments. A sales leader from a large enterprise software company might be exactly wrong for a product-led growth company that needs to build a sales organization serving customers who are already using the product. A product leader from a consumer internet company might be exactly the wrong fit for a developer tools company, where the go-to-market motion is fundamentally different.

The key is understanding what makes your business work specifically, codifying those success factors explicitly, and then building your scaled organizations to preserve what matters while adding the capabilities you need to grow. This requires resisting the temptation to simply hire experienced individuals and let them operate as they have before, trusting that experience at other companies translates automatically to your context.

Building Through Trust and Ethics

The companies that endure over decades are not those that optimize purely for growth or financial returns but those that build genuine trust with customers, employees, partners, and communities. Trust is built slowly through consistent behavior over extended periods and destroyed quickly by a single instance of betrayal or carelessness. In the short term, companies can often grow quickly by cutting corners, misleading customers, treating employees as disposable, or breaking commitments to partners. In the long term, these approaches create fragility and eventual collapse as reputations degrade and people choose alternatives.

Playing the long game means prioritizing trust, even when it constrains short-term growth or profitability. It means being honest with customers about what your product can and cannot do, rather than overpromising to close deals. It means honoring commitments to employees even when circumstances change, and it would be convenient to break them. It means treating partners fairly rather than extracting maximum value through power imbalances. It means acknowledging mistakes openly rather than covering them up or minimizing them.

This approach to business is not merely ethical in the abstract sense. It is strategically superior for building companies that compound value over decades. Trust reduces customer acquisition costs, as word-of-mouth and reputation drive organic adoption. Trust enables premium pricing as customers are willing to pay more for products and companies they trust. Trust enhances recruitment advantages, as talented individuals prefer to work for companies with strong reputations. Trust facilitates partnership opportunities, as other companies seek to align with trustworthy partners.

The challenge is that trust-building requires patience and consistency, which conflict with the incentive structures that dominate venture-backed startups. Investors typically want maximum growth as quickly as possible to maximize valuations for their next funding round or exit. This creates pressure to cut corners, to overpromise, to prioritize short-term metrics over long-term relationships. Founders who resist this pressure and are willing to grow more slowly to build more sustainably often face criticism from their boards.

Distribution as Enduring Moat

The final piece of playing the long game successfully is recognizing that distribution advantages are often the most defensible moats a company can build, more durable than product advantages or technological innovations that competitors can eventually match. Seen through the lens of compounding, distribution is not a function but an asset; one that strengthens with time rather than depreciating with use. Companies with superior distribution can win even when their products are not measurably better because they reach customers more effectively, retain them more successfully, and expand within accounts more efficiently.

Building distribution advantages that endure requires investing consistently over the years in channels and capabilities that take time to mature but become progressively stronger. Content libraries that drive organic search traffic compound as more content accumulates and earns authority. Brand recognition compounds as more people encounter the brand and form positive associations. Sales relationships compound as trust builds and your company becomes embedded in customer workflows. Partner ecosystems compound as more partners build on your platform and invest in the relationship.

These distribution advantages take years to build and cannot be quickly replicated by competitors with more capital or better products. A startup with superior technology cannot simply outspend an incumbent with years of accumulated content and search authority. A competitor with better product features cannot simply steal customers who have deep relationships with your sales team and extensive integrations with your platform. A well-funded new entrant cannot immediately replicate the community and ecosystem that has formed around the product over the years.

The strategic implication is that distribution should be understood not as a tactical concern but as, perhaps, the most important strategic question facing the business. Where you invest in distribution, how much you are willing to invest before seeing clear returns, and how patient you are in allowing distribution advantages to mature often determine whether you build an enduring company or a temporary success that is overtaken by competitors with more sophisticated distribution.

The Integration of Time and Strategy

Playing the long game is not about passivity or slowness. It is about recognizing that some advantages can only be built through sustained effort over extended time periods and being willing to make those investments even when the immediate payoff is unclear. Velocity and patience are not opposites; they are complements. Moving quickly to learn and iterate in the short term is what enables compounding advantages to form over the long term.

The companies that endure are built by founders who deliberately hold this tension. They operate with urgency in daily execution while maintaining restraint in where they invest attention and capital. They optimize for retention and expansion as much as acquisition, knowing that compounding requires a base that does not erode. They invest in distribution channels that take years to mature because they understand that distribution advantages separate temporary success from durable leadership.

This approach does not maximize valuation in the next funding round. It rarely produces explosive growth charts or clean narratives of overnight success. What it produces instead are businesses that strengthen as they scale, where progress accumulates rather than resets, and where growth creates advantage instead of fragility.

Playing the long game ultimately exposes a harder truth: time alone does not create durability. Endurance depends on whether growth produces leverage or merely magnifies effort. Many companies persist for years only to discover that scale has made them heavier, not stronger. What separates those outcomes is not ambition or patience, but architecture.

The Enduring Truth

Growth is not magic, luck, or genius, though all of those can help. Growth results from understanding how velocity creates momentum, how momentum enables sophisticated distribution, and how distribution advantages compound into lasting competitive moats. It is the result of making hundreds of correct decisions about where to invest time and capital, which opportunities to pursue and which to ignore, how to structure teams and organizations, and when to be patient and when to act with urgency.

The companies that win are not those that chase every trend or tactic, or a supposed shortcut to success. They are those that build real systems that generate value, that compound advantages over time, that get stronger rather than weaker as they scale. They are led by founders who understand that velocity matters but patience matters too, that moving fast and thinking long term are not contradictory but essential complements.

This is the path to building companies that matter, that last, that create genuine value for everyone they touch. It is more difficult than pursuing viral growth or optimizing for funding rounds. It requires greater discipline, greater strategic clarity, greater willingness to make difficult choices, and the ability to resist external pressure. However, it is the only path to building something genuinely enduring in a world where most startups fail, and most successes prove temporary. The long game is not about rejecting ambition or accepting slower growth. It is about channeling ambition toward advantages that strengthen with rather than decay under pressure.

Velocity opens doors. Momentum walks through them. Distribution turns that into a business. Patience, strategic clarity, and ethical consistency turn that business into something enduring. This is how companies become institutions, how startups become industries, how founders build legacies rather than just exits. The choice is always yours to make, in every decision, every day, throughout the entire journey of building something meaningful. Choose wisely and build well.

🔍 *Case Study - WeWork*

When Short-Term Thinking Destroys Long-Term Value

The cost of abandoning the long game is clearest when capital is abundant, ambition unchecked, and short-term signals mistaken for proof of durability. Few companies illustrate this more clearly than WeWork.

In 2010, when Adam Neumann and Miguel McKelvey founded WeWork in New York City, they entered the commercial real estate market with a vision that seemed to balance immediate execution with long-term transformation: create beautiful, community-oriented coworking spaces that would serve freelancers, startups, and increasingly remote workers who needed professional workspace more flexible than traditional office leases. The initial locations in SoHo demonstrated product-market fit, as the spaces filled quickly, members appreciated the aesthetics and community, and unit economics appeared viable with membership revenue exceeding rent and operating costs at mature locations.

Yet, what began as legitimate insight into changing work patterns and underutilized real estate transformed into a cautionary tale about how short-term thinking, disguised as visionary ambition, destroys value even when all three forces: velocity, momentum, and distribution, appear present. By 2019, WeWork had expanded to 800+ locations across 120+ cities in 37 countries, served 600,000+ members, achieved a $47 billion private valuation, and prepared for an initial public offering that would rank among the largest in technology history. Then the business model collapsed under scrutiny, revealing that velocity without viable economics is not velocity but expensive motion, that momentum without unit economic discipline is unsustainable, and that distribution without profitable scaling creates liabilities rather than assets.

VELOCITY WITHOUT ECONOMICS

WeWork's trajectory demonstrated how prioritizing growth metrics over unit economics creates an illusion of success that collapses when capital markets demand sustainable business models. The first critical mistake involved treating revenue growth and location expansion as primary success metrics while ignoring or obscuring the underlying economics that determined whether the business model could generate profits at scale. They expanded aggressively, signing long-term leases on expensive commercial real estate in premium locations, renovating spaces with high-end finishes and amenities, and marketing memberships at prices that filled locations quickly but did not cover the fixed costs and capital expenditures required to build out each space.

The expansion velocity was impressive by traditional startup metrics. They were adding dozens of locations per quarter, entering new cities monthly, and growing their membership base at rates that suggested inevitable market domination. But this velocity was funded through unsustainable economics: they signed 15-year lease obligations while selling month-to-month or short-term memberships, creating a massive maturity mismatch: long-term liabilities but short-term revenues.

When membership growth slowed or economic conditions shifted, they could not quickly reduce their lease obligations, turning their "asset-light" model into a liability-heavy reality. They also structured many leases with escalating rents over time, meaning their cost base would increase automatically even if membership revenue stagnated, and they provided membership guarantees to landlords in some cases, making them liable for minimum revenue regardless of actual occupancy.

The second critical failure involved optimizing for valuation multiples rather than sustainable profitability, treating WeWork as a technology platform deserving software-like valuations rather than a real estate business constrained by physical assets and lease obligations. Neumann and investors, including SoftBank's Vision Fund, embraced the narrative that WeWork was transforming the future of work through technology, community, and brand. This positioning justified technology company valuations of 10-20x revenue rather than real estate valuations of 1-2x revenue.

This narrative drove decision-making toward maximizing revenue growth even when unprofitable. They would subsidize membership prices to fill buildings quickly, offer generous perks and amenities that members valued but that destroyed margins, and expand into adjacent businesses like WeLive (co-living) and WeGrow (school) that consumed capital without improving core business economics. The technology narrative also justified corporate behavior antithetical to long-term value creation, including Neumann's self-dealing. He leased properties he personally owned to WeWork, trademarked the "We" name, then sold it to the company for $5.9 million, and borrowed against his equity stake to fund personal investments.

The third systemic problem involved creating governance and incentive structures that rewarded short-term growth over long-term sustainability. Neumann's super-voting shares gave him control despite mounting evidence that the business model was not viable at scale. Board oversight was weak despite the participation of sophisticated investors, including SoftBank, Benchmark, and JPMorgan, in funding rounds at escalating valuations.

Neumann's compensation and ego aligned with valuation growth rather than business fundamentals, creating perverse incentives in which he personally benefited from capital raises at higher valuations, even if those valuations were not justified by underlying economics. The executive team and employees were incentivized through equity grants based on the last-round valuation. This meant everyone's wealth depended on continuing the growth narrative, regardless of profitability, and internal financial reporting obscured losses through creative metrics like "Community Adjusted EBITDA," which excluded fundamental costs to present an illusory profitability.

COLLAPSE UNDER SCRUTINY

The execution unfolded across three phases that demonstrated how short-term thinking creates fragility that collapses when external conditions shift. The first phase, 2010 through 2017, represented genuine product-market fit and reasonable growth in the core coworking business. Early locations achieved profitable unit economics at maturity, membership demand validated the product vision, and expansion into major US and European cities made strategic sense given the rise of remote work. During this period, WeWork was building a legitimate business serving real customer needs, and while growth was aggressive, it was not obviously unsustainable. Many locations reached break-even within 18-24 months, and brand strength created a competitive moat against traditional executive suite operators and commodity office space.

The second phase, 2017 through mid-2019, represented the acceleration into unsustainable growth driven by SoftBank's Vision Fund investment and Neumann's ambition to become the world's first trillion-dollar company. They raised $4.4 billion from SoftBank in 2017 and additional billions in 2018-2019, using this capital to expand aggressively into secondary markets where demand was unproven, lease increasingly expensive flagship properties that would take longer to reach profitability, and diversify into adjacent businesses that diluted focus and consumed capital.

Revenue grew from $886 million in 2017 to $1.8 billion in 2018, and was projected to reach $3+ billion in 2019, creating the appearance of hypergrowth. But losses accelerated even faster. They lost $933 million in 2017, $1.9 billion in 2018, and were on pace to lose $3+ billion in 2019, demonstrating that scale was amplifying losses rather than creating profitability. The business model had shifted from "build profitable locations and expand" to "raise capital to fund unprofitable growth and hope scale eventually creates profits," and the capital markets' willingness to fund this model was reaching limits.

The third phase, August through October 2019, marked the collapse, as public market scrutiny exposed the unsustainable economics and governance problems that private investors had tolerated or ignored. When WeWork filed an S-1 for an initial public offering in August 2019, public market investors immediately questioned the business model: Why were losses growing faster than revenues? How would long-term lease obligations be managed if membership growth slowed? Why was corporate governance so weak? How was this different from the traditional real estate business despite the technology narrative?

Within weeks, the IPO roadshow encountered severe pushback, with investors declining to participate at valuations even a fraction of the $47 billion private valuation. In September, facing an untenable situation, WeWork postponed the IPO indefinitely. In October, Neumann was forced out as CEO, and SoftBank provided $9.5 billion in emergency financing to prevent the company from going bankrupt. The valuation had collapsed from $47 billion to under $8 billion, and ultimately, WeWork filed for bankruptcy protection in November 2023, having destroyed tens of billions in investor capital.

💡 THE LESSON

WeWork's failure validates this chapter's central argument that playing the long game requires discipline around unit economics and sustainable growth rather than optimizing for near-term valuation or growth metrics at any cost. Analyzing through the long-term thinking lens reveals how short-term optimization destroyed value: they had velocity in location expansion and membership growth but velocity without profitable unit economics is just burning capital faster; they had apparent momentum as each new location added revenue but momentum without retention and profitability is unsustainable; and they had distribution through landlord partnerships and brand recognition but distribution that creates long-term liabilities without corresponding profits is strategic liability not asset.

The case demonstrates that in capital-intensive businesses with long economic cycles, sustainable scaling requires profitable unit economics before aggressive expansion, and that investor capital can disguise unsustainable business models but cannot permanently subsidize them. Most critically for founders, WeWork illustrates that the three forces must be built on a foundation of viable economics: velocity means iterating toward profitability, not expanding before proving unit economics; momentum requires retention and increasing customer value, not just customer acquisition; and distribution must become progressively more efficient, not progressively more expensive.

Key Takeaways

Stripped of narrative and case detail, this chapter basically posits that:

- Scaling without losing velocity and momentum requires deliberate organizational design, such as maintaining small-team dynamics, limiting communication overhead, and building systems that preserve focus as complexity increases, rather than allowing diffusion to slow execution at scale.
- Trust and ethics are not constraints on growth but foundations for building durable businesses, as reputation and relationships compound over time, reducing the need for constant enforcement, persuasion, or repair.
- Playing the long game requires patience with market adoption curves and advantage accumulation, while maintaining urgency in daily execution, optimizing for what compounds over decades rather than what merely impresses in quarters, even under sustained short-term pressure.

Playing the long game ultimately exposes a harder truth: time alone does not create durability. Endurance depends on whether growth produces leverage or simply magnifies effort. Many companies persist for years only to discover that scale has made them heavier, not stronger. What separates those outcomes is not ambition or patience, but architecture.

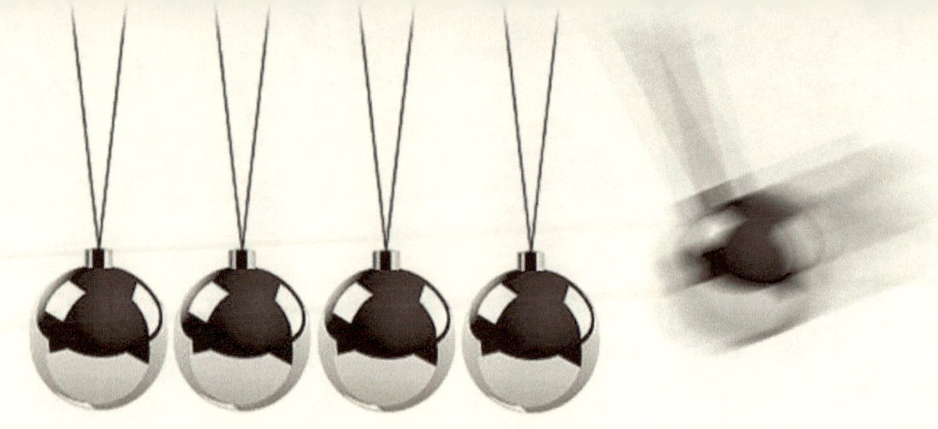

Chapter 11

The Architecture of Scale

Companies that scale efficiently do so not by adding resources proportionally to output but by building leverage into every system so that each unit of input produces progressively more output over time.

— Hoffman and Yeh, Ability to Scale

Scale Is Not an Additive Problem

Most founders view scale as an additive problem. When customer demand exceeds capacity, add more servers. When support volume exceeds the team's capacity, hire additional support staff. When the sales pipeline grows beyond what existing reps can handle, expand the sales organization. This approach to scaling treats growth as fundamentally linear, in which each increment in output requires a proportional increase in input. Companies built on this model can grow, sometimes substantially, but they never achieve the kind of leverage that transforms good businesses into exceptional ones.

The architecture of scale determines whether a company can grow without proportionally increasing complexity, whether margins expand or contract as volume increases, and whether the business becomes progressively more valuable or merely larger. Getting this architecture right requires understanding what creates leverage, where to invest in building scalable systems, and how to sequence those investments so that each enables the next stage of growth rather than optimizing prematurely for scale that has not yet arrived.

The Nature of Operational Leverage

Operational leverage exists when incremental transactions or customers require minimal incremental cost to serve. Software companies achieve this naturally to some degree because serving additional users costs far less than acquiring and onboarding the first users. The marginal cost of one more software license or one more user on a platform approaches zero, though this overstates the case because customer acquisition, support, and infrastructure all have real costs that scale with growth. Yet the fundamental economics remain favorable in ways that distinguish software from businesses in services or physical goods.

However, not all software businesses achieve operational leverage to the same extent. A SaaS product that requires extensive manual onboarding, custom configuration for each customer, and ongoing high-touch support has fundamentally different unit economics than one with self-service signup, standardized configuration, and automated support systems. Both are software businesses, but only the latter has architected true operational leverage into the business model. The difference compounds dramatically over time. At ten customers, the distinction might seem minor. At 1,000 customers, it determines whether the company is profitable or incurring capital losses due to operational overhead. At 10,000 customers, it often determines whether the company can survive without raising substantial additional capital to fund the operational complexity.

Building operational leverage requires intentional decisions about product design, customer experience, and business model structure. Products must be designed for self-service wherever possible, not because high-touch sales and service are inherently wrong, but because they limit scale unless serving premium segments where economics justify the cost. Customer onboarding must be streamlined to the point where new users can extract value quickly without extensive handholding. Support systems must progressively shift from reactive ticket handling to proactive issue prevention through better product design, clearer documentation, and community-driven assistance.

These are not merely operational improvements but strategic imperatives that determine scalability. Companies that fail to build operational leverage find themselves trapped in patterns in which growth requires proportional increases in headcount, margins remain compressed regardless of volume, and the business never generates the cash flow to support reinvestment in product and market expansion. They grow but never scale, increasing revenue without increasing value or creating sustainable advantages.

Technology Infrastructure as Foundation

Technology infrastructure decisions made during early development compound over time, either enabling rapid scaling or creating technical debt that becomes progressively more expensive to address. Founders often underestimate the extent to which early architectural choices constrain subsequent options because the consequences remain hidden until growth exposes limitations. A database architecture that works perfectly for thousands of users becomes unmanageably slow at hundreds of thousands. A monolithic codebase that enables fast iteration when the team is small becomes impossible to modify safely when multiple teams need to ship features simultaneously. An infrastructure designed for one geographic region requires complete rebuilding to support global expansion.

The challenge is that companies that scale efficiently treat infrastructure as a strategic asset that enables capabilities rather than merely as a technical foundation that supports features. They deliberately invest in infrastructure that creates leverage, in which improvements benefit multiple use cases and enable future capabilities that are difficult to predict precisely but follow from general directions.

Infrastructure decisions that typically create the most problematic long-term constraints include data models that cannot evolve as product requirements change, integration approaches that tightly couple systems in ways that prevent independent scaling or replacement, security and privacy architectures that cannot meet enterprise requirements without fundamental rebuilding, and deployment processes that limit how quickly changes can ship safely. These are not merely technical considerations but business constraints because they directly limit velocity, determine what markets you can serve, and affect how quickly you can respond to competitive threats or market opportunities.

Perfect infrastructure is impossible, and attempting it wastes resources. Adequate infrastructure that does not limit next-stage growth while maintaining velocity is the realistic goal.

Strategic Process and Automation

Process and automation occupy an interesting position in how companies scale because they can either enable growth or stifle it, depending on when and how they are introduced. Too much process too early kills the velocity and flexibility that early-stage companies need to find product-market fit and adapt to market feedback. Too little process, too late, creates chaos as coordination failures multiply and knowledge exists only in individual heads rather than in systems that allow scaling beyond the founding team. The question is not whether to introduce process but when and how to do so in ways that create leverage rather than overhead.

The right time to introduce process is at inflection points where the absence of process begins to limit velocity, rather than at a predetermined company size or headcount threshold. When the same questions get asked repeatedly, that signals the need for documented answers that are easily discoverable. When coordination failures cause delays or errors, that signals the need for clearer ownership and communication protocols. When onboarding new team members takes weeks because knowledge transfer happens ad hoc, that signals the need for systematic training materials and onboarding processes.

Automation follows a similar logic but with a different threshold. Manual processes are often optimal when you are still learning what the right process should be because automation locks in approaches before you have validated they are correct. However, manual processes limit scalability because they require proportional increases in headcount to handle higher volume. The right time to automate is when the process is well understood and stable, when the volume justifies the investment, and when manual execution is becoming a bottleneck that limits growth.

The most valuable automation is not what eliminates the most labor but what creates the greatest leverage by enabling capabilities that would be impossible to achieve manually. Automated testing enables much faster shipping because developers can make changes confidently without extensive manual validation. Automated deployment enables continuous delivery, significantly reducing the time from code completion to customer value. Automated monitoring and alerting enable operating at scale without proportional increases in operations headcount because problems are detected automatically rather than through customer reports or manual checks.

Companies that scale view process and automation as tools for creating leverage rather than as bureaucratic requirements or cost-reduction measures. They introduce process deliberately when it solves real problems and enables growth. They strategically automate when it creates capabilities or removes bottlenecks, rather than merely reducing labor costs. They maintain the discipline to keep processes minimal and to focus automation on what matters most, rather than allowing overhead to accumulate simply because resources are available to build systems.

Unit Economics and the Path to Leverage

Unit economics determine whether a business can scale profitably or whether growth merely accelerates cash burn without creating a path to sustainable profitability. The fundamental question is whether serving each additional customer generates more value than it costs to acquire and serve that customer, and whether those economics improve or deteriorate as the business scales.

The mistake many founders make is accepting poor unit economics, assuming they will improve naturally as the business scales. Sometimes this is correct. Customer acquisition costs often decrease as brand awareness builds and word-of-mouth becomes a more significant acquisition channel. Infrastructure costs per customer typically decrease as fixed costs are spread across larger customer bases. Support costs per customer can decrease as self-service resources improve and community support reduces demand for company-provided assistance.

But unit economics can also deteriorate with scale. Customer acquisition costs sometimes increase as you exhaust the most accessible segments and must reach less-qualified or more-expensive audiences. Infrastructure costs can increase if the product was not designed to scale efficiently or if serving larger customers requires more resources per user. Support costs can increase if product complexity grows faster than self-service capabilities or if serving enterprise customers requires more extensive handholding than serving smaller customers.

The companies that scale most efficiently design for unit economics from the outset by understanding what drives customer acquisition cost, lifetime value, and cost to serve, and then build systems that improve each as the business grows. They structure pricing to capture greater value from customers who derive more value from the product, rather than charging uniformly across segments with very different willingness-to-pay profiles. They invest in product improvements that reduce the support burden and enable self-service, rather than scaling support teams in proportion to customer growth. They build acquisition channels that have favorable economics at scale rather than relying on approaches that work when you are small but become prohibitively expensive as you grow.

This requires understanding not only current unit economics but also how they are likely to evolve as the business scales, and what investments are necessary to ensure they improve rather than deteriorate. It requires making deliberate choices about which customer segments to serve, which product capabilities to develop, and which distribution channels to invest in, based on their long-term economic potential rather than their immediate contribution to growth. It requires discipline to forgo revenue opportunities with poor unit economics, even when growth targets create pressure to accept any customer at any price.

Organizational Structure as Scaling Architecture

The architecture of scale encompasses not only technology and operations but also organizational design, which determines how effectively teams can work as the company grows. Small teams achieve remarkable velocity because everyone has context, decisions happen quickly without extensive coordination, and information flows naturally through frequent interaction. As companies grow, these advantages erode unless organizational structure is deliberately designed to preserve them even as headcount increases.

The traditional approach to organizational design focuses on creating hierarchies and reporting structures that establish clear authority and accountability. This is necessary to some degree as companies grow, but it is not sufficient for maintaining velocity, because hierarchies increase coordination overhead, slow decision-making by adding approval layers, and fragment ownership, making it unclear who is responsible for outcomes. Companies that scale while maintaining velocity do not simply layer hierarchies; instead, they create organizational structures that preserve small-team dynamics even within larger organizations.

This typically entails structuring the organization around autonomous teams that own specific outcomes and have the authority and resources to achieve them without constant coordination with other teams. It means minimizing dependencies between teams so that one team's velocity is not limited by another team's capacity or priorities. It means establishing clear interfaces and contracts between teams so that coordination happens through well-defined mechanisms rather than ad hoc negotiation, which consumes time and energy.

The specific organizational structure matters less than whether it enables teams to maintain velocity while minimizing coordination overhead. Some companies organize around customer segments, others around product areas, and others around technical domains. What matters is whether teams have clear ownership, whether they can make decisions and execute independently, and whether the structure minimizes the need for cross-team coordination that slows everything down.

As organizations grow, the temptation is to add more process, more approvals, more coordination mechanisms to prevent problems. Each addition makes sense in isolation, but collectively they create bureaucracy that kills velocity. The alternative is to invest in systems that enable distributed decision-making by ensuring that teams have the context, resources, and authority they need to act independently. This includes shared metrics and dashboards that make performance visible, clear strategic priorities that guide decision-making without requiring constant consultation with leadership, and documented principles that help teams make consistent choices without extensive discussion.

The architecture of scale ultimately determines whether growth creates leverage or merely adds complexity. Companies that understand this invest deliberately in building systems, infrastructure, and organizational structures that enable each stage of growth to occur more efficiently than the previous one. They focus not on optimizing for where they are, but on building the foundation that will enable them to be where they need to be. They make choices that compound favorably over time, even when simpler alternatives would be adequate for current needs. This is how companies transform from startups that struggle to scale into enduring businesses that grow efficiently and sustainably across years and decades.

🔍 *Case Study - Grab*

When Organizational Architecture Enables Regional Dominance

In 2012, Anthony Tan and Tan Hooi Ling founded Grab (initially as MyTeksi) in Kuala Lumpur, Malaysia. They entered Southeast Asia's ride-hailing market with the recognition that the region's fragmentation, 8 diverse countries with different languages, regulations, currencies, consumer behaviors, infrastructure maturity, and competitive dynamics, created a unique scaling challenge, where organizational architecture would determine winners more than product superiority or capital access. Southeast Asia represented a massive opportunity with 650+ million people, a rapidly growing middle class, increasing smartphone penetration, and transportation infrastructure that created perfect conditions for ride-hailing disruption.

Yet, the regional diversity meant strategies that worked in one market often failed in others: Singapore's high-income, high-regulation environment required a different approach than Indonesia's price-sensitive, cash-based economy; Thailand's entrenched taxi interests created regulatory challenges absent in Vietnam; and the Philippines' archipelagic geography demanded different operational solutions than Malaysia's road-connected urban centers. Companies that treated Southeast Asia as a single market with a standardized playbook consistently underperformed local competitors who adapted to market-specific realities, while companies that operated country subsidiaries as independent businesses failed to capture regional synergies in technology development, capital efficiency, and network effects.

DECENTRALIZED EXECUTION, CENTRALIZED INFRASTRUCTURE

Grab's approach demonstrated how organizational architecture can maintain velocity while adding momentum by balancing local autonomy with regional coordination. The first architectural principle involved decentralizing execution authority to country-level teams who understood local market dynamics, competitive threats, regulatory environments, and consumer preferences. Each country had a general manager with P&L responsibility who could make decisions about pricing strategies, driver incentive programs, marketing campaigns, partnership priorities, and product feature adaptations without requiring approval from regional headquarters.

This decentralization prevented the coordination bottlenecks that plague centrally-managed regional businesses: when the

Indonesia team identified an opportunity to integrate cash payments before other markets were ready for this complexity, they could move quickly without waiting for regional consensus. When Singapore faced new regulations requiring driver training certifications, the local team could implement compliance systems tailored to specific requirements. When Thailand's competitive dynamics demanded aggressive driver subsidies in specific cities, country leadership could deploy capital tactically without bureaucratic approval processes that would delay response.

The second architectural principle involved centralizing core infrastructure, such as technology platforms, data systems, payment processing, fraud detection, customer support tools, and driver allocation algorithms, thereby creating economies of scale and enabling knowledge transfer across markets. Rather than each country building its own technology stack, Grab invested in shared systems that provided a foundation for local customization: all markets used the same core ride-hailing platform, with configuration options for local payment methods, languages, and features. All markets benefited from shared fraud detection algorithms that learned from patterns across the region. All markets could deploy features that have been successfully tested elsewhere with minimal additional development cost.

This centralization created compounding advantages that decentralized competitors could not match: when one market's engineering team built a better driver navigation system, all markets could deploy it. When data scientists improved demand forecasting algorithms using Indonesian data, those improvements benefited Singapore and Malaysia. When product managers developed food delivery features for Thailand, other markets could launch food delivery faster because the core platform already existed. Competitors operating as independent country businesses had to rebuild these capabilities separately, creating cost disadvantages and slower iteration velocity.

The third architectural principle established clear interfaces between centralized and decentralized functions, preventing ambiguity about decision authority while enabling efficient coordination. Core platform engineering reported to the regional CTO, who prioritized technology investments serving multiple markets, but each country had a local engineering team that could customize the platform for market-specific needs. Regional finance managed treasury, capital allocation, and investor relations, but country general managers controlled operational budgets and P&L. The regional policy team negotiated with governments and regulatory bodies, but local teams managed day-to-day compliance and operational licensing.

These interfaces meant decisions happened at the appropriate level: strategic technology architecture that affected all markets required regional coordination to prevent fragmentation, but tactical product features serving specific market needs could move at local velocity. Capital allocation decisions balancing investment across markets required a regional perspective, but operational spending within approved budgets stayed local. Regulatory frameworks affecting multiple markets benefited from a coordinated regional approach, but operational compliance could adapt to local enforcement realities without waiting for regional consensus.

SCALING WITHOUT PROPORTIONAL COMPLEXITY

The execution unfolded across three phases that demonstrated how proper organizational architecture enables complexity to grow linearly rather than exponentially with scale. The first phase, 2012 through 2015, established the foundational architecture while building initial market presence in Malaysia, Singapore, Thailand, Vietnam, Indonesia, and the Philippines. During this period, they tested the centralized infrastructure model by building a core platform that multiple markets could deploy, validated that country-level P&L authority enabled faster local decision-making than competitors' regional matrix structures, and learned which functions needed regional coordination (technology, data, capital) versus local autonomy (operations, marketing, partnerships).

The competitive landscape included well-funded rivals: Uber was expanding aggressively across the region with a standardized global playbook, local competitors like Go-Jek in Indonesia had home-market advantages, and numerous smaller players operated in specific countries. Grab's architectural advantage became evident as they could move with local velocity. This included adapting to cash payments in Indonesia faster than Uber's credit-card-first approach, partnering with local taxi companies in markets where this made strategic sense, and customizing driver incentives to local competitive dynamics. They also benefited from regional scale advantages in technology development, fraud prevention, and capital efficiency.

The second phase, 2015 through 2018, tested whether the architecture could maintain velocity while expanding service offerings beyond core ride-hailing into food delivery (GrabFood), package delivery (GrabExpress), digital payments (GrabPay), and financial services (insurance, lending). Each vertical required local customization, restaurant partnerships worked differently across markets, payment regulations varied dramatically, delivery logistics faced different infrastructure constraints, but a centralized platform enabled faster multi-vertical expansion than building separate businesses.

The architectural advantage compounded: when GrabFood launched in Thailand and proved product-market fit, other markets could deploy food delivery using the same core platform with local restaurant partnerships and menu curation. When GrabPay integrated with Indonesian e-commerce platforms, the technical infrastructure could extend to Malaysian retail partnerships. When fraud detection algorithms learned patterns from ride-hailing, they could protect food delivery and payments with minimal additional development. Competitors who had built single-vertical businesses faced much higher costs and longer timelines to expand into adjacent verticals because they lacked shared infrastructure.

The third phase began around 2018 when Grab's super-app strategy demonstrated that organizational architecture had become a sustainable competitive moat. They announced the acquisition of Uber's Southeast Asian operations, eliminating a major competitor while acquiring technology assets and market share. They expanded to 500+ cities across 8 countries, serving tens of millions of users across multiple service verticals. They raised funding at a $14+ billion valuation, reflecting investor confidence that their architecture enabled efficient scaling.

Most critically, they could enter new markets or launch new services with a fraction of the cost and time required by competitors: adding a new country to the platform meant deploying existing infrastructure with local operational setup, not building technology from scratch. Launching a new vertical meant extending the shared platform, not creating a separate business unit. This architectural advantage meant their expansion costs decreased over time, while competitors' costs remained constant or increased, a classic example of how proper architecture creates momentum, making future growth easier than past growth.

By 2021, when Grab went public via a SPAC merger at a $40 billion valuation, they were processing billions of transactions annually, operating in 8 countries, serving 187 million users, and had built an ecosystem connecting drivers, merchants, financial services partners, and logistics providers that would be nearly impossible for competitors to replicate. This success reflected organizational architecture that enabled complexity to scale linearly: adding 8th country created less organizational overhead than adding second country because shared infrastructure absorbed most complexity, launching fourth vertical required less incremental cost than launching second vertical because platform was designed for multi-service operation, and managing 500 cities was more efficient than managing 100 cities because centralized systems automated coordination that would otherwise require proportional headcount growth.

💡 THE LESSON

Grab's trajectory validates this chapter's central argument that the architecture of scale means designing organizational structures that maintain velocity while adding momentum, enabling complexity to grow linearly rather than exponentially. Analyzing through the organizational architecture lens reveals how structural choices created sustainable advantages: decentralized execution preserved velocity because country teams could adapt to local market dynamics without coordination bottlenecks; centralized infrastructure created momentum because technology investments and operational learnings compounded across markets rather than fragmenting into redundant efforts; and clear interfaces between central and local functions prevented ambiguity while enabling efficient coordination at appropriate decision levels.

The case demonstrates that in multi-market platform businesses, organizational architecture becomes the primary determinant of scaling efficiency. Companies with superior architecture can expand faster, cheaper, and more sustainably than competitors with comparable products or capital because their structure enables growth without a proportional increase in complexity. Grab illustrates that architecture of scale requires deliberate design from early stages: decisions about what to centralize versus decentralize, how to structure decision authority, and where to establish coordination interfaces compound dramatically as organizations grow, and retrofitting proper architecture after reaching scale is far more difficult than building it correctly from the beginning.

Key Takeaways

The structural logic that determines whether growth makes a company lighter or heavier over time can therefore be summarized thus:

- Operational leverage is what separates scalable businesses from labor-intensive ones: systems are built so that additional customers cost little to serve, and unit economics improve, rather than merely growing revenue through effort.

- Early architectural decisions compound. Technology, organization, processes, and business model choices either enable efficient scaling or create debt that makes growth heavier, slower, and more complex over time.
- Process and automation should be introduced strategically at inflection points where manual approaches begin limiting velocity, rather than prematurely optimizing for scale that has not yet arrived

At scale, the challenge shifts outward. Systems and leverage may be in place, but competitors respond, markets adapt, and yesterday's advantages quietly erode. The final chapter looks at how competitive pressure really plays out, and what it takes to keep building advantage as the game keeps changing.

Chapter 12

Competitive Dynamics and Sustainable Advantage

Markets are never static, and competitive advantages
erode continuously unless you are building new
advantages faster than existing ones decay, requiring
perpetual investment in compounding capabilities
that competitors cannot easily replicate.

— Michael E. Porter, Competitive Advantage

Competitive Advantage is Not Static

The concept of competitive advantage occupies a central place in strategic thinking about business. Yet, the way most founders and executives think about advantage is static and defensive, failing to reflect how competition actually works in fast-moving markets.

The traditional framing focuses on building moats that protect market position, on creating barriers that prevent competitors from replicating what has been built, and on establishing positions that can be defended over the long term. This perspective made sense in industries where change happened slowly and established positions could be protected for decades through patents, economies of scale, or regulatory capture.

In technology markets characterized by rapid change, low barriers to entry, and constant innovation, static advantages erode quickly, and defensive thinking leads to complacency rather than sustained leadership.

The companies that maintain competitive positions over the years do so not by building impregnable moats but by continuously building new advantages faster than existing advantages decay. They think offensively about capabilities they need to develop rather than defensively about positions they need to protect. They understand that competitive advantage is not something you establish once but must actively maintain through sustained investment in capabilities that competitors cannot easily replicate.

This requires understanding which types of advantages are most durable, how competitive dynamics differ across market structures, when to respond to competitive threats and when to ignore them, and how to build differentiation that creates space to develop advantages without direct comparison to established alternatives. It requires accepting that no advantage lasts forever and that the goal is not permanence but sufficient duration to build the next advantage before the current one erodes completely.

The Half-Lives of Different Advantages

Not all competitive advantages decay at the same rate. Understanding which advantages are durable and which are ephemeral helps allocate investment appropriately, focusing resources on building advantages with longer half-lives rather than temporary barriers that provide only brief protection.

Product features represent the most ephemeral form of advantage because they can typically be replicated by competent competitors once their value is demonstrated. Feature advantages matter early, enabling differentiation and initial traction, but they rarely sustain leadership. Companies that succeed long term use feature advantages to buy time to build more durable advantages before imitation occurs.

Pricing advantages are similarly fragile. Competitors can match pricing if they choose, either by accepting lower margins or by achieving cost structures that enable sustainable lower prices. Competing primarily on price advantages, the competitor with the deepest pockets or lowest costs wins. Unless pricing reflects a fundamental cost advantage that competitors cannot match, pricing advantages disappear quickly.

Brand and reputation are more durable because they must be earned through consistent delivery over time. Strong brands reduce acquisition friction, create pricing power, and insulate companies from competitive noise. However, brand advantages erode if quality declines or customer experience deteriorates, and competitors can build brands through sustained excellence.

Distribution and network effects are the most durable advantages because they create structural barriers that persist even when competitors build comparable products.

Superior distribution determines whether any other advantage can reach the market. Network effects create self-reinforcing flywheels in which each new user increases value for existing users. Even these advantages erode eventually as channels shift or new platforms emerge, but they decay far more slowly than features or pricing.

The most durable advantages are those that compound continuously, where leadership today enables even stronger positions tomorrow through mechanisms competitors cannot easily replicate.

Offensive Capabilities vs. Defensive Moats

The defensive moat metaphor is useful but incomplete because it emphasizes protection over progress and static position over dynamic capability. Moats matter when competitors attempt direct replication, but in fast-moving markets, the primary threat is often indirect: competitors solving the same problem in a fundamentally different way.

In these environments, defensive barriers provide only limited protection because disruption can arrive from unexpected directions. The companies that maintain leadership do so through offensive capabilities that enable continuous innovation rather than static defenses. They invest in product development, customer understanding, and execution velocity to move faster than competitors, rather than relying on barriers that slow everyone equally.

Offensive capabilities compound over time. Each improvement generates data, insight, and momentum that enable the next improvement. Each market expansion provides resources and learning that facilitate future expansion. Talent density and organizational alignment increase execution speed in ways competitors struggle to match.

This creates a different form of advantage: one based on velocity and momentum rather than protection. The advantage lies not in secrecy or barriers, but in the organizational capability to execute consistently at high speed and quality. Competitors can see what you are doing and still be unable to replicate it.

Market Structure and Winner-Take-All Dynamics

Competitive dynamics vary dramatically with market structure, yet founders often assume all markets are winner-take-all. This assumption encourages aggressive land grabs, justifies poor unit economics, and treats every competitor as an existential threat.

Winner-take-all dynamics exist, but only under specific conditions. Strong network effects, substantial economies of scale, or high switching costs can create outcomes where leadership becomes self-reinforcing. Social networks, operating systems, and cloud infrastructure often exhibit these dynamics.

Many markets lack these characteristics and support multiple successful companies with different positioning, segments, or geographic focus. Consumer markets rarely converge on a single winner. B2B markets often sustain multiple providers because customers value alternatives, and solutions vary by context.

Understanding market structure fundamentally changes strategy. In winner-take-all markets, growth and share justify aggressive investment. In multi-winner markets, differentiation, unit economics, and sustainable positioning matter more than scale at any cost. Assuming winner-take-all dynamics where they do not exist leads to poor decisions that sacrifice durability for growth that does not compound.

Strategic Response to Competition

Every competitor move creates pressure to respond, but responding indiscriminately dilutes focus and turns strategy into imitation. Matching features, prices, or expansions by default gradually erodes differentiation, leaving competition to devolve into execution efficiency or price wars.

The alternative is strategic selectivity: responding to threats that undermine core advantages while ignoring noise that does not materially affect position. Most feature launches do not require a response because they do not change switching behavior. Chasing them diverts resources from building differentiated strengths.

Pricing moves are especially difficult. Matching unsustainable price cuts sacrifices margin without solving the underlying problems. When competitors burn capital to buy market share, ignoring them is often the correct response. When competitors have genuine cost advantages, the response is differentiation and segmentation, not price matching.

The discipline to ignore non-threatening moves is difficult but essential. Sustainable advantage comes from deliberate strategy, not reactive behavior.

Differentiation as Strategic Foundation

The strongest competitive position comes from doing different things rather than doing the same things better.

Competing head-to-head invites direct comparison on dimensions where incumbents often have advantages. Differentiation creates space where comparison is difficult and where advantages can be built without matching competitors across every dimension.

Differentiation can emerge through product approach, customer segment focus, or business model design. The strongest differentiation aligns with underserved customer needs and with organizational strengths that competitors struggle to replicate because doing so would conflict with their existing models or structures.

Building sustainable advantage requires accepting continuous erosion and investing offensively in capabilities that enable renewal. It requires a calibrated market strategy, selective responsiveness to competition, and differentiated positions that provide room to compound advantages over time.

🔍 *Case Study - Spotify*

When All Three Forces Create Defensible Position Against Better-Resourced Competitors

In 2006, when Daniel Ek and Martin Lorentzon founded Spotify in Stockholm, Sweden, they entered the digital music market at a moment when the industry was simultaneously collapsing and transforming. CD sales were declining precipitously due to piracy. iTunes had established paid downloads as a legitimate alternative but suffered from fragmentation, where users owned scattered collections rather than accessing comprehensive catalogs, and streaming services like Pandora offered internet radio but not on-demand listening.

The founding vision focused on creating a legal streaming service that was more convenient than piracy, more comprehensive than download ownership, and more personalized than internet radio, solving user problems while addressing record labels' need for a legitimate monetization channel.

Yet by 2008, when Spotify launched broadly in Europe, and 2011, when it entered the US, the competitive landscape included, or would soon include, vastly better-resourced rivals. Apple Music (launched 2015), with 1 billion iOS devices, provided built-in distribution, and the iTunes ecosystem provided existing customer relationships. Amazon Music (launched in 2007, rebranded as Prime Music in 2014), with 200+ million Prime subscribers, offered music as a membership benefit and used pricing power to subsidize user acquisition. YouTube (which had launched a music-focused service) had billions of users, a free ad-supported model, and video content that music-only services could not match. Also, numerous well-funded startups were attempting variations on the streaming model.

The standard strategic analysis suggested Spotify would struggle to compete. They lacked Apple's distribution advantage of default apps on every iPhone, Amazon's ability to bundle music with existing membership and lose money to gain share, YouTube's free model and video content, and the financial resources to outspend these technology giants in content licensing or user acquisition. Yet, Spotify not only survived but thrived, reaching 500+ million users and 200+ million paying subscribers by 2024, maintaining market leadership in music streaming despite facing competitors with structural advantages in distribution, pricing, and content. Their success demonstrated that sustainable competitive advantage requires all three forces: velocity, momentum, and distribution, working together continuously, and that no moat is permanent without constant reinvestment across all three areas.

BUILDING DEFENSIBILITY THROUGH INTEGRATED FORCES

Spotify's approach demonstrated how sustainable advantage comes from velocity, momentum, and distribution reinforcing each other rather than relying on a single competitive strength. The first force involved velocity through continuous product innovation that kept user experience improving faster than competitors could copy features. They pioneered personalized playlists, like Discover Weekly, Release Radar, and Daily Mixes, which used listening history and collaborative filtering to surface music that users would love but had not discovered. They built social features that let users share playlists, see what friends were listening to, and collaborate on music curation. They developed podcast integration that transformed Spotify from a music app to a comprehensive audio platform.

This innovation velocity created a competitive moat because competitors could not copy individual features. Apple Music launched personalized playlists, YouTube added music recommendations, and Spotify's continuous iteration kept the experience gap. When competitors copied Discover Weekly, Spotify had already launched Release Radar. When rivals built social features, Spotify had moved to podcast integration. The velocity advantage was not that any single feature was impossible to replicate, but that the pace of improvement meant competitors were always catching up rather than leading, and users who valued the best audio discovery experience had reason to prefer Spotify even when alternatives were cheaper or better distributed.

The second force involved momentum through personalization that created switching costs and improved with scale. Every song played, every playlist created, every skip or replay told Spotify's algorithms more about user preferences, enabling progressively better recommendations. This created a compound effect where long-term users received increasingly personalized experiences that would be lost if they switched platforms. For example, their Discover Weekly playlist would not exist on Apple Music because Apple would not have their listening history. Their Daily Mixes would reset to generic recommendations on YouTube Music. Their year-end summary disappeared from Amazon Music.

This personalization moat strengthened over time and scaled with the user base: more users meant more data for training recommendation algorithms, improving personalization for everyone. More listening history per user led to better individual recommendations, boosting retention. The momentum from personalization strengthened Spotify's competitive position through tenure and scale. Newer services or services with fewer users could not match Spotify's recommendation quality, and users who switched lost the personalization they had built up. Competitors with comparable algorithms still could not replicate this advantage without stealing Spotify's user data, and regulations like GDPR prevented the transfer of listening history between platforms.

The third force involved distribution through creator relationships and platform integrations, making Spotify increasingly hard to displace. They invested heavily in podcast exclusives and creator tools, acquiring Anchor (podcast creation), Megaphone (podcast advertising), and exclusive rights to popular podcasts like Joe Rogan Experience. That made Spotify the destination for podcast listeners, even if they preferred competing services for music. They integrated with smart speakers, car entertainment systems, gaming consoles, and smart TVs, becoming the default music service in contexts where competitors were unavailable or not primary options.

They also built the Spotify for Artists platform, providing musicians with analytics, promotion tools, and direct fan communication channels, thereby creating creator lock-in in which artists promoted their Spotify presence because the platform offered better tools than competitors. This distribution through creator relationships meant users came to Spotify for specific podcasts or artists who promoted their presence there, and creators brought audiences that Spotify had not directly acquired. The distribution advantage compounded as more creators chose Spotify as their primary platform, bringing their audiences, which attracted more creators in a virtuous cycle that competitors struggled to disrupt.

COMPETING AGAINST STRUCTURAL ADVANTAGES

The execution unfolded across three phases that demonstrated how V ∩ M ∩ D creates defensibility against single advantages that individually seem insurmountable. The first phase, 2008 through 2015, established Spotify's position before major tech platforms fully committed to music streaming. During this period, they focused on building the best music discovery experience through personalization algorithms, expanding geographic availability through complex label negotiations, and creating a freemium model that drove conversion from ad-supported to premium subscriptions.

The early competitive landscape included Pandora, with a strong US presence but limited on-demand capabilities; Rdio, with a similar model but less effective execution; and various local streaming services in different markets. Spotify's advantage came from superior product execution, better recommendations, stronger social features, and better desktop and mobile apps, combined with disciplined geographic expansion and a freemium model that grew the user base while converting a meaningful percentage of users to paid subscriptions. By 2015, when Apple Music launched, Spotify had 75 million users, including 20 million paying subscribers, established brand recognition, and momentum that made it difficult to displace despite Apple's distribution advantages.

The second phase, 2015 through 2019, tested whether Spotify's model could withstand direct attacks from technology giants with structural advantages. Apple Music launched as the default app on every iPhone, with deep iOS integration, 3-month free trials to convert iTunes customers, and $10/month pricing that matched Spotify. Amazon launched Prime Music, included with Prime membership, and later Amazon Music Unlimited as a standalone service, leveraging pricing power to offer family plans at $15/month (compared to Spotify's $15) and single-device Echo plan at $4/month. YouTube doubled down on music with YouTube Red (later YouTube Premium), offering ad-free music and video, and YouTube Music as a dedicated music app.

Each competitor had advantages Spotify could not match: Apple controlled the OS platform and could integrate music deeply into operating system features, Siri voice assistance, and the Apple Watch. Amazon could bundle music with a Prime membership valued at $100+/year for other benefits, making music seem "free." YouTube had video content that music-only services lacked and could offer a free ad-supported tier that competed with Spotify's freemium model while monetizing through video ads. Yet, Spotify maintained market leadership by ensuring all three forces worked together: they kept product innovation velocity high with podcast expansion and personalization improvements that made the experience demonstrably better than competitors; they leveraged momentum through personalization and listening history that created switching costs rivals could not overcome; and they expanded distribution through smart speaker integrations, car entertainment partnerships, and creator relationships that made Spotify available everywhere and promoted by influential podcasters and musicians.

The third phase began around 2019 when Spotify's sustained growth despite overwhelming competitive pressure validated that V ∩ M ∩ D creates a defensible position that single advantages cannot replicate. They went public in 2018 via direct listing at a $26.5 billion valuation, demonstrating investor confidence in sustainability despite competitive threats. They reached 500 million total users and 200+ million paying subscribers by 2024, maintaining clear market leadership in music streaming even as Apple Music reached 100+ million subscribers and Amazon Music served 80+ million customers.

Most critically, they demonstrated that sustainable advantage requires continuously rebuilding all three forces rather than defending static position: they maintained velocity through podcast acquisitions, audiobook integration, and AI-powered features that kept experience improving; they compounded momentum through personalization that became increasingly accurate with more data and longer user tenures; and they expanded distribution through partnerships that made Spotify ubiquitous across devices, platforms, and creator ecosystems. Competitors who focused on a single advantage: Apple's distribution, Amazon's pricing, and YouTube's free tier could not overcome integrated defense, where velocity, momentum, and distribution reinforced each other.

THE LESSON

Spotify's trajectory validates this chapter's central argument that sustainable competitive advantage comes from all three forces working together continuously, and that no moat is permanent without constantly rebuilding velocity, momentum, and distribution. Analyzing through the competitive dynamics lens reveals how integrated forces created defense against structural disadvantages: velocity through continuous product innovation meant user experience stayed ahead of better-resourced competitors who could copy individual features but not pace of improvement; momentum through personalization created switching costs and improved with scale, making long-term competitive position stronger over time; and distribution through creator relationships and platform integrations made Spotify increasingly difficult to displace even when alternatives were pre-installed, bundled, or free.

The case demonstrates that in technology markets where competitors have structural advantages in capital, distribution channels, or existing customer relationships, sustainable advantage requires building defensibility across multiple dimensions that reinforce each other. Most critically for founders, Spotify illustrates that $V \cap M \cap D$ creates exponential defensibility: the intersection of all three forces provides protection that any single force cannot, and maintaining competitive position requires continuously rebuilding each force because competitors will attack wherever you are weakest. Resting on past advantages means inevitable displacement when better-resourced rivals focus resources on your market.

Key Takeaways

A few structural truths govern how advantage is built, eroded, and renewed:

- Competitive advantages decay at different speeds: features and pricing fade quickly, while distribution and network effects endure, making sustained advantage a product of continuously building new capabilities rather than defending static positions.
- Winner-take-all outcomes arise only under specific conditions, such as strong network effects, high switching costs, and economies of scale, whereas most markets support multiple durable winners with distinct positioning.
- Effective competitive response requires discernment, not reflexes; reacting to every move erodes focus, while responding only to real threats preserves strategic leverage.
- The strongest competitive positions come from doing different things, not doing the same things better, because differentiation creates space where advantages can grow without direct comparison.

Competitive advantage is less something you hold than something you keep rebuilding. Markets move, competitors adapt, and strengths decay. The companies that endure are not those that defend positions longest, but those designed to renew advantage as a matter of course.

Extras:
A Set Theory Perspective on Startup Growth

Imagine three overlapping circles. A Venn diagram where each circle represents one of the fundamental forces of growth: **Velocity, Momentum, and Distribution.**

Each force exists independently, but the real power lies in their intersections.

The Three Sets In Relation to Startup Growth

Set V: Velocity

The set of all activities that increase learning speed, iteration cycles, and execution pace. This includes:

- Rapid product releases
- Fast customer feedback loops
- Quick experimentation cycle
- Agile decision-making processes
- Short time-to-market intervals

Companies operating purely in Set V move fast but may lack

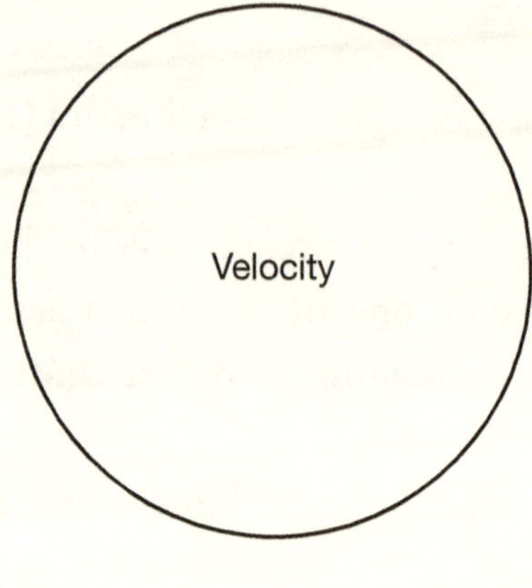

Set V: Velocity

direction or compounding advantages. They sprint without necessarily building anything that lasts.

Set M: Momentum

The set of all activities that create compounding advantages over time. This includes:

- Product improvements that increase retention
- Network effects that strengthen with scale
- Brand equity that accumulates
- Customer relationships that deepen
- Market position that reinforces itself

Companies operating purely in Set M build gradually but

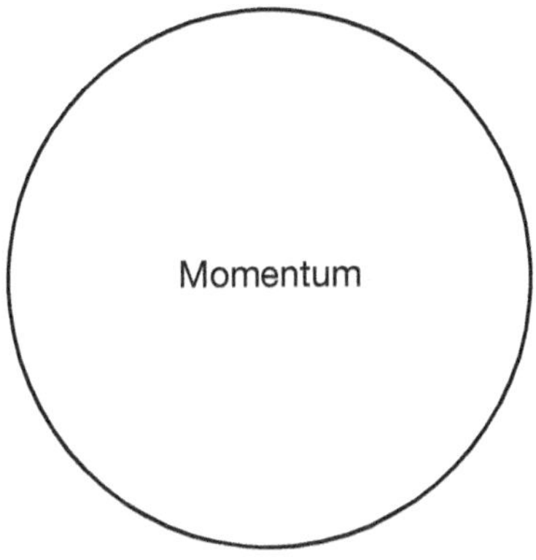

Set M: Momentum

may move too slowly to capture market opportunities or respond to competitive threats.

Set D: Distribution

The set of all systematic advantages in reaching and acquiring customers. This includes:

- Owned channels (email lists, user bases, content libraries)
- Platform relationships and partnerships
- SEO and organic discovery mechanisms
- Sales infrastructure and processes
- Brand recognition and word-of-mouth systems

Companies operating purely in Set D can reach customers

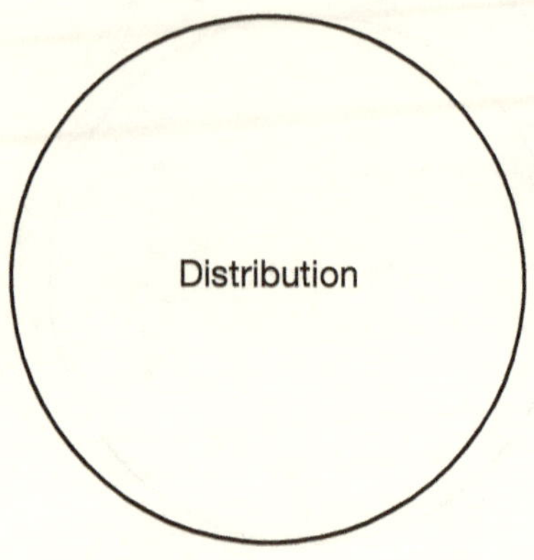

Set D: Distribution

efficiently but may lack product velocity to iterate or momentum to retain them.

The Intersection: Where Magic Happens

V ∩ M (Velocity + Momentum, without Distribution)

Fast compounding, but limited reach

Companies here iterate rapidly while building compounding advantages, but struggle to scale because they have not solved the distribution problem.

Example: A B2B SaaS company with exceptional product

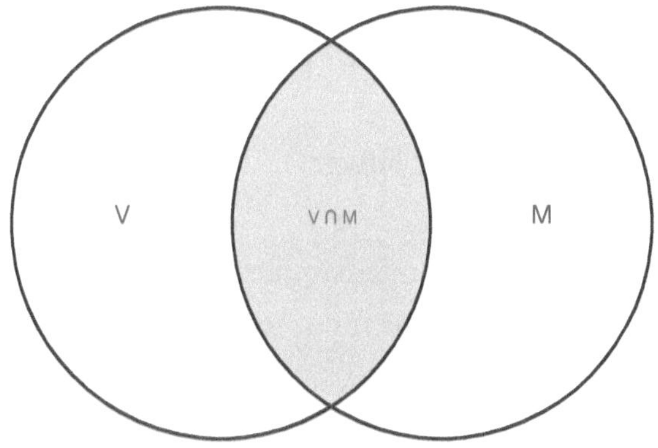

V ∩ M : Velocity ∩ Momentum

velocity and strong retention metrics (90%+ annual retention) but no systematic way to acquire customers beyond founder-led sales. They build better and better products for a small, loyal customer base, but cannot break through to the next growth tier.

The product improves quickly (velocity), customers stay and expand (momentum), but growth remains linear because each new customer requires manual effort (missing distribution).

V ∩ D (Velocity + Distribution, without Momentum)

Fast reach, but no staying power

Companies here can acquire customers efficiently and iterate quickly, but cannot retain them or build compounding advantages.

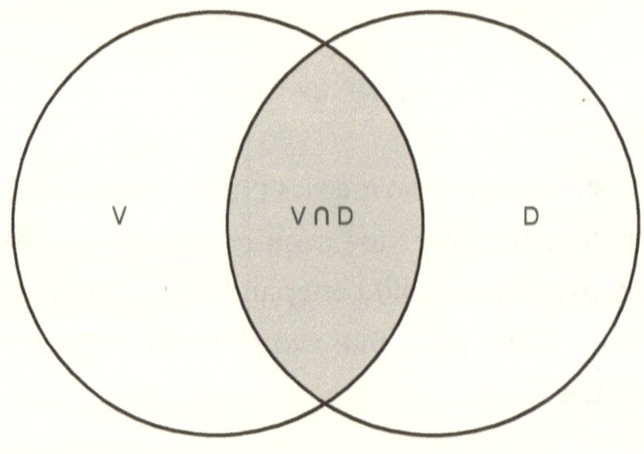

V ∩ D : Velocity ∩ Distribution

Example: A consumer app that excels at paid acquisition and rapidly deploys features but has poor retention. They continually acquire new users to replace churned users, running faster just to stay in place.

They reach customers efficiently (distribution) and iterate quickly on features (velocity), but users do not stick around long enough to create network effects or word of mouth (missing momentum).

M ∩ D (Momentum + Distribution, without Velocity)

Strong fundamentals, but too slow

Companies here retain customers well and have systematic distribution advantages, but move too slowly to capitalize on opportunities or defend against faster competitors.

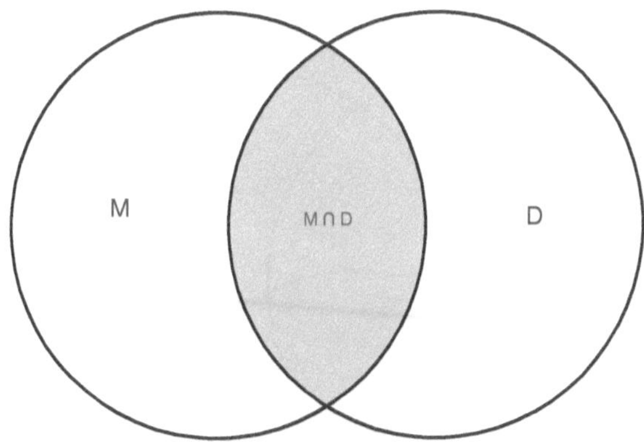

M ∩ D : Momentum ∩ Distribution

Example: An established company with strong brand recognition and loyal customers that takes 18 months to ship major features. They have distribution channels that work and customers who stay, but competitors out-innovate them because they cannot iterate fast enough.

They retain customers well (momentum), reach them efficiently (distribution), but lose market position to faster-moving competitors (missing velocity).

The Center: V ∩ M ∩ D

The Growth Triforce

The intersection of all three sets is where sustainable, explosive growth happens.

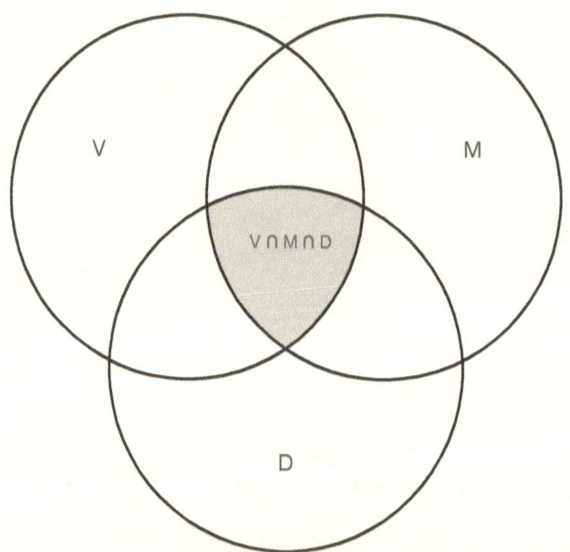

V ∩ M ∩D : Velocity ∩ Momentum ∩ Distribution

Companies operating in this center space:

- Iterate rapidly to find what works (Velocity)
- Build compounding advantages that strengthen over time (Momentum)
- Scale customer acquisition through systematic channels (Distribution)

Example: An AI startup during its growth phase, shipping features while maintaining strong retention, launching strategic partnerships with OpenAI, Anthropic, Meta, Apple, Amazon, NVIDIA, and Perplexity (distribution), iterating weekly on product features (velocity), and building network effects as more teams adopted the platform (momentum).

Another example: A fintech startup scaling from 10,000 to 450,000 users, running rapid experiments across multiple paid channels (velocity + distribution), building product features that increased retention (momentum), and creating word-of-mouth growth as users invited others (momentum + distribution).

The Empty Spaces: What Lies Outside

Outside all three sets

Companies that lack any of these forces struggle to grow. They move slowly, do not retain customers, and have no systematic way to reach new ones. These companies rarely survive long enough to matter.

The null set ($\emptyset$)

This represents the absence of growth entirely: the startup that never launches, never iterates, never acquires a single customer. It exists only in theory.

Set Cardinality: Size Matters

Not all implementations of velocity, momentum, or distribution are equal. The cardinality (size) of each set matters.

$|V|$ = The magnitude of your velocity advantage
Small $|V|$: Shipping quarterly
Large $|V|$: Shipping daily with structured experimentation

$|\mathbf{M}|$ = The strength of your compounding advantages
Small $|\mathrm{M}|$: 60% annual retention
Large $|\mathrm{M}|$: 95% retention + expanding revenue per customer + network effects

$|\mathbf{D}|$ = The scale of your distribution advantages
Small $|\mathrm{D}|$: Founder-led sales only
Large $|\mathrm{D}|$: Owned channels + partnerships + viral loops + brand + SEO

Growth rate is proportional to: $\mathbf{G} \propto |\mathbf{V}| \times |\mathbf{M}| \times |\mathbf{D}|$

Companies with large values across all three dimensions grow exponentially. Companies with small values in any dimension face constraints.

Subset Relationships: How The Forces Build On Each Other

Velocity $\subset$ Momentum

Velocity is actually a prerequisite for momentum. You cannot build compounding advantages without the ability to iterate and improve. Every element of momentum requires velocity to be created in the first place.

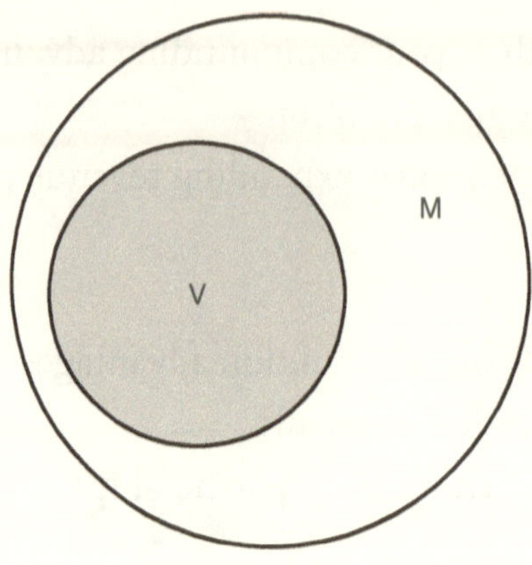

V ⊆ M : Velocity ⊆ Momentum

You cannot build retention without iterating on the product. You cannot create network effects without shipping the features that enable them. Velocity is the engine; momentum is what velocity creates when applied consistently over time.

Distribution ⊂ (Velocity ∪ Momentum)

Effective distribution requires either velocity (to quickly test channels) or momentum (to create word-of-mouth and organic growth). Distribution advantages are built, not found—and building them requires either speed of iteration or compounding product value.

Paid acquisition requires rapid testing (velocity). Organic growth requires product value that generates word-of-mouth (momentum). Partnership distribution requires either fast integration capability (velocity) or a market position that makes you attractive (momentum).

Union vs. Intersection: The Strategy Choice

V ∪ M ∪ D: **Having any one force**

This is the minimum viable company—you have at least one advantage. Many startups operate here, excelling in one dimension while struggling in others.

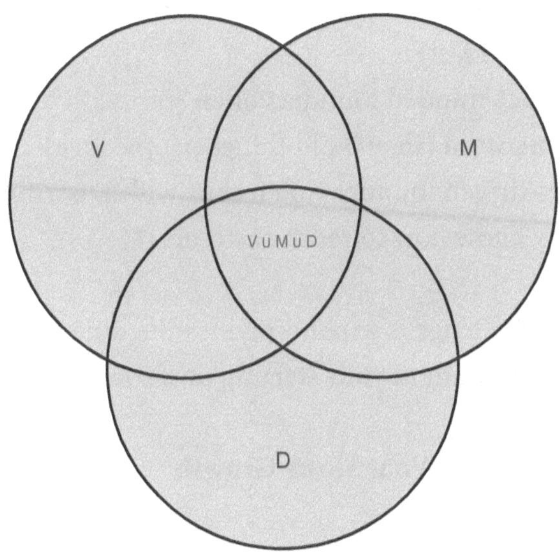

V ∪ M ∪ D : Velocity ∪ Momentum ∪ Distribution

$V \cap M \cap D$: **Having all three forces simultaneously**

This is the compounding-growth company—where each force amplifies the others, and growth becomes exponential rather than linear.

The strategic question every startup faces: **How do we move from the union to the intersection?**

Most companies start strong in one set:

- Technical founders often start with **Velocity** (they can build fast)
- Product-minded founders often start with **Momentum** (they build things people love)
- Sales-driven founders often start with **Distribution** (they know how to reach customers)

The growth challenge is expanding into the other sets while maintaining strength in your starting position.

The Complement: What Slows Growth

For each set, there exists a **complement** — the set of all things that work against that force:

V' (not Velocity): Slow decision-making, bureaucracy, technical debt, analysis paralysis

M' (not Momentum): High churn, commoditized products, weak retention, no compounding advantages

D' (not Distribution): Dependency on single channels, no owned audience, purely transactional customer relationships

Companies fail when **(V' ∪ M' ∪ D')** becomes large—when they accumulate more obstacles than advantages.

Practical Application: Mapping Your Position

Draw three circles. Honestly assess where your company sits:

1. **Are you in V?** Can you ship weekly? Do you run structured experiments? Do you make decisions in days, not months?
2. **Are you in M?** Are customers staying? Is revenue per customer growing? Are you building advantages that compound?
3. **Are you in D?** Do you have systematic ways to reach customers? Are you building owned channels? Do customers bring other customers?
4. **Where are the intersections?** Which combinations are you achieving? Which are you missing?
5. **What is your cardinality?** Even if you are in all three sets, how strong is your position in each?

The goal is not perfection across all dimensions immediately. The goal is understanding which set you are strongest in, which intersections you have achieved, and which gaps represent your highest-leverage growth opportunities.

The Final Equation

If we represent startup growth as a function:

Growth = f(V, M, D)

Then successful growth is not: **G = V + M + D** (additive)

But rather: **G = V × M × D** (multiplicative)

When any variable approaches zero, growth approaches zero, no matter how strong the others are. When all three are present and growing, the effects multiply.

The Venn diagram indicates that growth is not about choosing among velocity, momentum, and distribution. It is about systematically moving your company toward the center where all three forces overlap and amplify each other.

That intersection is where billion-dollar companies are built.

Epilogue:

The Compounding Advantage

The central argument of this book can be stated simply: startups succeed not through singular, brilliant insights or fortunate timing, but through the systematic accumulation of advantages that compound through velocity, momentum, and distribution. The difficulty lies not in understanding the concept but in maintaining the discipline to execute consistently over the years when the path is unclear and when the pressure to compromise long-term value for short-term metrics becomes overwhelming.

Every founder who has built something meaningful has faced moments where the right long-term decision conflicted sharply with the expedient short-term choice. The moment when investing more capital in inefficient acquisitions would produce growth metrics that unlock the next funding round, but would also establish unsustainable unit economics. The moment when promising features the product cannot deliver would close important deals, but also damage trust.

These moments reveal character and determine trajectories. Companies that consistently prioritize short-term expediency eventually find themselves trapped in patterns they cannot escape, burdened by technical or operational debt and suffering reputational damage. Companies that consistently prioritize long-term value creation build foundations that become progressively stronger and more defensible.

The Myth of the Optimal Path

One of the most persistent and damaging myths in startup culture is the notion that successful companies follow an optimal path that can be studied, codified, and replicated. This myth manifests in blog posts analyzing how specific companies achieved growth and in frameworks that promise playbooks for similar results.

The reality is messier and more contingent. Every successful company navigated unique circumstances, made decisions based on incomplete information, benefited from fortunate timing in some dimensions while struggling in others, and succeeded despite numerous mistakes. The path that worked for one company will not work for another, and attempting to follow someone else's playbook often leads to strategic confusion.

This does not mean that studying successful companies is worthless. It means that the patterns that matter are more abstract and more fundamental than the specific tactics companies follow. The useful lessons concern how companies approached problems rather than which solutions they implemented.

Understanding velocity, momentum, and distribution as the fundamental forces that drive growth provides a more useful framework than studying specific growth tactics, because these forces operate consistently across contexts.

Building for Uncertain Futures

One of the defining characteristics of startups is operating under conditions of fundamental uncertainty, in which the future cannot be predicted with confidence and the market itself is still being defined. This uncertainty makes planning difficult, yet it does not eliminate the need for strategy.

This suggests thinking about strategy less in terms of specific goals and more in terms of positioning and optionality. Instead of committing fully to a narrow vision of the company's future, maintain flexibility to adapt as conditions evolve. Instead of betting everything on a single distribution channel or business model, develop multiple paths to market.

The companies that endure are not those that perfectly predicted the future. They are those who maintained sufficient velocity to learn quickly, built enough momentum to adapt when conditions changed, and developed distribution advantages that gave them staying power.

The Human Dimension

Throughout this book, the focus has been primarily on systems, mechanisms, and strategic frameworks. Yet reducing startup success purely to systems misses the essential human dimension that ultimately determines whether companies succeed or fail.

Behind every successful company are human beings making difficult decisions under stress, maintaining conviction when outcomes are uncertain, and finding the psychological resources to persist through setbacks. The systems matter, but they operate through human judgment, creativity, and resilience.

The founder's role is ultimately less about having brilliant insights and more about creating the conditions where talented people can do exceptional work together. It is about building teams that trust one another enough to take risks and be candid about problems.

The most important quality a founder can cultivate is self-knowledge of their strengths, weaknesses, biases, and blind spots. Understanding where your judgment is reliable and where you systematically make errors is essential.

The Privilege and Responsibility of Building

Starting a company is an enormous privilege that relatively few people have the opportunity to pursue. It requires access to resources that remain unavailable to most of the world, and it remains far more accessible to some people than to others, largely due to circumstances beyond individual control.

This privilege carries responsibility for how you build, who benefits from what you create, and what kind of world your work contributes to building. A narrow focus on growth at all costs often externalizes costs onto workers, communities, and society as a whole.

Playing the long game means expanding the definition of success beyond financial returns to include the broader impact of what you build. The choices you make in the early stages establish patterns and culture that become progressively harder to change as the organization grows.

The Work Continues

This book has attempted to provide frameworks for understanding how growth works and for engineering it through velocity, momentum, and distribution. These principles provide guidance, but they do not eliminate the difficulty of execution or the uncertainty of outcomes.

Navigating this complexity requires combining strategic clarity with tactical flexibility. It requires conviction about your direction while remaining open to evidence that you need to change course. The founders who succeed are not those who avoid mistakes or execute flawlessly. They are those who learn quickly from inevitable mistakes and have the resilience to persist through setbacks.

The Final Word

Velocity creates options through rapid learning and iteration. Momentum creates compounding advantages through consistent execution. Distribution creates defensibility through accumulated relationships, brand, and systematic advantages.

Yet, understanding these forces intellectually is only the beginning. The real challenge is sustaining execution over the years. This is hard work that will test everything you have. But this is also work that matters. Building companies that solve real problems creates value that compounds through the economy.

This is the work. It has always been the work. Understanding the principles changes how you approach it, but does not make it easier. The opportunity is there for those willing to do the work. The rest is up to you. Build something that matters. Build something that lasts. Build something that makes the world genuinely better.

Exclusive Free Startup Strategy Session

If you have read this book, you already understand what drives sustainable growth. This is an opportunity to apply it directly to your company.

I am offering a one-off free 15-minute private strategy session for readers who want to put the Velocity, Momentum, and Distribution framework into action in their startup or organization.

In this session, we will:

- Diagnose where your growth is constrained across Velocity, Momentum, and Distribution;
- Identify which forces (or intersection) will unlock the most leverage right now; and
- Translate the framework into concrete, executable next steps for your product, growth, or go-to-market strategy.

Scan the QR code to book your session.

Time slots are limited and reserved exclusively for readers of this book. Put the three forces to work. Build momentum that compounds.

Join the Three Forces Circle

This book is not meant to end on the page. It is meant to be applied through real decisions, real teams, and real constraints.

The Three Forces Circle is a private community for readers who want to turn the Velocity, Momentum, and Distribution framework into action in their companies.

Inside the Circle, members get:

- Direct access to Velocity, Momentum, and Distribution application guides, tools, and working frameworks
- Invitations to private events and live workshops
- A complimentary 15-minute strategy session
- Preferred pricing on future books, workshops, and team sessions

Membership also unlocks exclusive reader-only benefits, including:

- Up to 25% off future book releases and events
- Up to 40% off live team workshops

Once you join, you will receive a personal access key and choose how you want to engage: learning, applying, or pressure-testing the framework in your own context.

Scan the QR code to join
the Three Forces Circle
on Slack

ACKNOWLEDGMENTS

This book exists because of conversations and experiences that changed how I think about building companies.

To the founders who shared their stories with uncommon candor: Your willingness to discuss not just what worked, but what didn't, and more importantly, why, transformed abstract patterns into concrete understanding. The frameworks in this book emerged from your experiences, your mistakes, and your hard-won insights.

To my early readers who challenged every assertion, who forced me to prove causation rather than correlation, who caught every instance where I confused tactics with systems. This book is sharper because you refused to let lazy thinking pass.

To the venture capitalists who opened their pattern libraries: The best investors don't just fund companies; they study why outcomes diverge from expectations. Your willingness to share what you've learned from both successes and failures, often anonymously, made this book possible.

To the researchers and journalists who documented these companies in real time: Your contemporaneous accounts proved invaluable for understanding their decisions in their original context, before hindsight bias rewrote the narrative.

To my dear editor, Queenette, who understood that this project required forensic depth rather than inspirational breadth. Your patience made it three times easier and better.

To my family: Abigail, Emem, and Uwakmfon, thank you for being a stronghold and for putting up with me so I could get this book completed. And to Mom and Dad, who taught me to question conventional wisdom and follow the evidence.

To the founders currently building: You won't find shortcuts in these pages. What you will find is a framework for making better decisions, understanding structural forces, and building companies designed to compound. That's harder than growth hacking, and more valuable than any viral moment.

AUTHOR'S NOTE

This book analyzes companies using public information: published interviews, regulatory filings, and journalistic reporting. Where founders or employees shared perspectives directly, I note that explicitly. Where reasoning is inferred from observable actions, I label it as interpretation.

I have no financial interest in the companies discussed as primary case studies. While I have consulted for technology companies, none featured here are ones I have worked with. This distance allows for analysis without the need to defend outcomes or narratives.

On Survivorship Bias:

Like all case-based work, this book is subject to survivorship bias. For every company that successfully built velocity, momentum, and distribution, many others attempted similar approaches and failed. Success is never the product of structure alone; execution, timing, market conditions, and yes, luck, all matter.

On Evolving Landscapes:

Technology markets evolve faster than books can keep up. Some companies analyzed here may stumble after publication; others may emerge as better examples. That does not invalidate the framework. The goal is to understand forces that persist even as specific players change. So, where possible, this book emphasizes decisions made years ago, where outcomes can be evaluated with some distance. The framework matters more than any single company.

On Prescriptive Advice:

Nothing in this book should be read as prescriptive instruction. Strategies that worked for Monzo, Stripe, or Spotify were deeply contextual. Blind imitation is cargo-cult thinking. When specific decisions are discussed, they are used to illustrate principles, not provide templates. The task is to understand why something worked, then reason carefully about what that means in your own context.

On Definitions:

Velocity, momentum, and distribution are used here with deliberate precision. These terms are often conflated in startup discourse, obscuring important distinctions that should be separated. Separating them is essential to understanding how growth compounds and why it so often fails to.

On Omissions:

This book does not attempt to cover every dimension of building a company. Fundraising, hiring, culture, and many other topics are not discussed here because, although they matter deeply, they deserve focused treatment of their own. The scope here is intentionally narrow: the structural interaction of velocity, momentum, and distribution, because it is both underexplored and foundational.

On Certainty:

I have written with confidence because excessive hedging makes ideas unusable. That confidence is analytical, not predictive. The framework explains why certain structural decisions created advantages in the past. It does not promise future success. The goal of this book is not to give answers, but to help you ask better questions. Build accordingly.

On Feedback:

This framework is intended for application in real operating environments. If you encounter errors, stronger counterexamples, or structural flaws in the reasoning, I welcome that feedback.

The most valuable critique comes from people actively building companies and making decisions under constraint. You can share feedback at *www.edidiongekong.com*

ABOUT THE AUTHOR

Edidiong Ekong is a growth leader, entrepreneur, and author whose work over the past 10 years has focused on building growth systems that scale across stages, markets, and business models. His experience spans companies moving from first traction to category leadership, where growth is less about tactics and more about compounding advantage.

He has held senior growth and product marketing roles at multiple venture-backed companies, including Fireflies.ai, where he led product marketing and go-to-market strategy for major launches. This included Talk to Fireflies (developed in partnership with Perplexity), the launch of over 200 AI Apps, and strategic partnerships with OpenAI, Anthropic, Zoho, WhatsApp, Slack, and n8n, through which he aligned product strategy, distribution, and narrative to support go-to-market execution at scale.

Earlier in his career, Edidiong designed and executed rapid experimentation frameworks at Payday across Facebook Ads, Google, Spotify, Snapchat, and Twitter. These systems helped grow the platform from 10,000 to over 450,000 users and positioned the company for acquisition.

At Boomplay, he led growth in Nigeria during a period of intense competition, expanding the user base from 9 million to 60 million in under 2 years while maintaining market leadership against global platforms including Spotify, YouTube Music, and Apple Music.

At Alerzo, he drove the expansion of Alerzoshop and Alerzopay to more than 150,000 businesses across 16 cities, contributing to $250+ million in annual revenue.

Beyond operating roles, Edidiong has advised founders in Y Combinator and Techstars-backed companies, including Bujeti, LaborHack, OurPass, CRAND Technology, Herconomy, OnePort365, and Maplerad. His work has consistently focused on helping teams convert early momentum into durable growth systems rather than short-term gains, resulting in combined business value exceeding $5 billion.

His work centers on identifying the mechanisms that allow growth to compound across products, channels, and markets, beyond individual initiatives such as launches, experimentation, partnerships, and market expansion.

Edidiong currently teaches Product Marketing at AltSchool Africa, a Techstars-backed education company, where he focuses on market research, customer segmentation, positioning, and product launches, bridging theory with lessons drawn directly from practice.

He holds a master's degree in International Marketing from the University of Dundee (UK), an MBA in E-commerce from Nexford University (US), and a Bachelor's degree in Mathematics from the University of Uyo, though most of what appears in this book came from conversations with founders who were building companies while he was theorizing about them.

He believes the best business books forensically examine what happened and why, leaving readers to determine what that means for their own context. He believes most business books fail this standard, including probably this one, in ways he can't yet see.

He lives in London, where he continues researching how companies build compounding advantages in markets that resist them.

This is his first book. Whether it's his last depends on whether it's useful.

Feel free to reach out:

www.linkedin.com/in/edidiongekong

www.x.com/edidiongmekong

www.instagram.com/edidiongekong/

www.medium.com/@edidiongekong

www.edidiongekong.com

www.ingramcontent.com/pod-product-compliance
Lightning Source LLC
Chambersburg PA
CBHW020912060726
47591CB00004B/1200